19th-Century Patchwork Divas'

Treasury of Quilts

10 Stunning Patterns,
30 Striking Options

Betsy Chutchian and Carol Staehle

Martingale®
Create with Confidence

19th-Century Patchwork Divas' Treasury of Quilts:
10 Stunning Patterns, 30 Striking Options
© 2016 by Betsy Chutchian and Carol Staehle

Martingale®
19021 120th Ave. NE, Ste. 102
Bothell, WA 98011-9511 USA
ShopMartingale.com

Printed in China
21 20 19 18 17 16   8 7 6 5 4 3 2 1

Library of Congress Cataloging-in-Publication Data
is available upon request.

ISBN: 978-1-60468-795-8

MISSION STATEMENT

We empower makers who use fabric and yarn
to make life more enjoyable.

CREDITS

PUBLISHER AND
CHIEF VISIONARY OFFICER
Jennifer Erbe Keltner

CONTENT DIRECTOR
Karen Costello Soltys

DESIGN MANAGER
Adrienne Smitke

MANAGING EDITOR
Tina Cook

COVER AND
INTERIOR DESIGNER
Regina Girard

ACQUISITIONS EDITOR
Karen M. Burns

LOCATION PHOTOGRAPHER
Adam Albright

TECHNICAL EDITOR
Laurie Baker

STUDIO PHOTOGRAPHER
Brent Kane

COPY EDITOR
Durby Peterson

ILLUSTRATOR
Lisa Lauch

SPECIAL THANKS
*Thanks to the following home owners in Des Moines, Iowa,
for generously allowing us to photograph in their homes:*
Jason Clayworth and Joe Clark
Doug Kouma
Rick and Sue Frambach
Karla Conrad

CONTENTS

Introduction

As the 19th-Century Patchwork Divas' block-exchange group approaches a milestone anniversary of 20 years, our thoughts turn to our inception and how we've grown, both in numbers and knowledge.

The year was 1997 and we (Betsy and Carol) had talked for some time about getting a few of our quilting friends together to exchange blocks based on our common interests in 19th-century quilts, blocks, and fabrics. We began with a small, enthusiastic group of 12 members and one rule: to make our blocks using only 1800s reproduction fabrics, which were just beginning to appear on the market. Judie Rothermel's first Civil War fabric line was the inspiration for our first exchange. Along with fabrics from the era, we also drew ideas for our exchanges from member-owned antique quilts and tops, from single antique blocks, and from information and photos of 19th-century quilts found in published books. There was so much inspiration!

Because our group was small, we easily managed as many as four block exchanges a year for many years. That may not seem like a large number of exchanges, but the purpose of the group isn't just to exchange blocks; we also want to create quilts from the blocks received in the exchanges. Members design the majority of those quilts, often inspired by antique quilts.

Participation in the exchanges is voluntary, so the number of participants varies with each one. Occasionally we offer two exchanges at the same time. For instance, one exchange involved the Sunflower block, which used acrylic templates that some members found too challenging. At the same time, we also offered a paper-foundation-pieced Sunburst block. The two styles appealed to nearly all in the group, and some members participated in both!

Since 1997, our group has grown to 24 members, and during that time the fabric industry's range of reproduction fabrics has also increased. With so many more fabric options, we became more definitive in our choice of fabric colors and prints to suit the time period of the quilts we wished to re-create. Our sources for antique quilts also expanded to include state quilt-documentation books, which provide abundant inspiration for replicating quilts from the 1800s.

As the years have passed, we've slowed down the pace of the exchanges and now do about two a year. Perhaps it's due to older eyes or older fingers or even the arrival of grandchildren, or maybe it's because we're interested in more complex and challenging blocks that require more time to reproduce. Regardless, we may not be keeping the pace with which we began, but as of this writing, our enthusiasm hasn't diminished and we've completed more than 50 exchanges since the group started. We gather every July for an annual retreat where we sew, visit, and have a fantastic show-and-tell of all sorts of quilts, not just ones from our block exchanges. While we're all together, we take the opportunity to discuss future exchanges. We gather again in December for an exchange and Christmas party.

This book is the next step in our journey. After almost 20 years of exchanges, we still have a passion for reproduction fabrics, wonderful traditional quilts, and our sister Divas, and we want to share our quilts with others who might have the same aspiration of establishing a 19th-century block-exchange group. Even if you want to go it alone or skip the formalities of a structured group and just get a few friends together for a single exchange, this book will provide great inspiration and patterns for beautiful quilts.

Within the following pages, you'll find blocks of various levels of difficulty. A simple Ohio Star block can be as exciting to exchange as a more complex Wild Goose Chase block. Originality blossoms in the settings for each exchange.

Each chapter includes step-by-step instructions for one quilt based on the featured block, plus a gallery of three additional quilts using different settings. Ten blocks and 40 quilts are set before you to inspire you to gather friends, start your own group, and discover the pleasure the 19th-Century Patchwork Divas have enjoyed for nearly 20 years and hope to enjoy for years to come. Enjoy the process! A beautiful and bountiful stack of blocks awaits.

~ *Betsy and Carol*

While you can make all the blocks for any quilt by yourself, why not share the work and the fun with a group of friends? Here are our best Patchwork Diva tips for having a fun and successful exchange. Of course, beginning with this book as your guide simplifies everything. But, here's how our group begins.

1. Gather a group of friends with the same quilting interest and similar sewing skills. Look at quilts in your area of interest, whether they're actual quilts or photos. Discuss and share ideas about blocks you want to make.

2. For each exchange, decide on the block you'd like to create. You can do this by voting as a group, letting the group leader decide, or giving each member a turn to decide. If you have out-of-town members that aren't present to see the inspiration quilt, consider an online group through which you can share.

3. Once you've selected the block, set guidelines regarding the fabric colors, time period, and finished sizes of the block and quilt. Be specific.

4. Based on the quilt size, determine how many blocks are needed to make a quilt. Divide that number by the number of participants to see how many sets of blocks each person needs to make. For example, if the number of blocks needed for each quilt is 48, and there are 12 members

participating, each person will make four sets of 12 blocks, with each set made from a different fabrics to keep things scrappy.

Don't feel you're required to have a sizable group for a successful exchange. Patchwork Divas often do sub-exchanges, usually because they want more than the agreed number of blocks. A small group may prefer a different time frame as well, such as completing a block or two every week or several blocks a month, instead of setting one due date for all the blocks.

5. Set a due date and get a firm commitment from those who wish to participate. Once your date is set, consider setting a dropout date. We all sew at a different pace and have different schedules for sewing time, but if someone drops out after the number of sets has been calculated, everyone else in the group must then make up for the missing blocks or the quilt plan will have to change. Respect your fellow members. Don't wait until the last minute to get started. Of course, we can't plan for the unexpected, so in those situations, be flexible and considerate.

6. Establish a leader for each exchange. This person distributes block patterns and guidelines, and keeps a record of the participants, due dates, and so on. Encourage everyone to keep a notebook of patterns, inspirations, and names and addresses of members.

At the start of the exchange, it's extremely helpful for someone to make one block to show to the group. The block will build interest, and by making one block, the person can give construction and pressing tips as well as guidance on specific colors to include or exclude.

7. As a group, set your own rules. Yes, you need them; adhering to a set of rules makes everyone happy in the long run. Our number-one rule is to make and give the quality of work we wish to receive. Other items to consider can be the thread color, seam allowance width (scant ¼" or true ¼"), direction to press the seam allowances, and most importantly, whether or not to prewash fabrics—everyone has to agree on this one.

Every so often, the Patchwork Divas need a break from blocks with triangular shapes. A Postage Stamp quilt, a longtime favorite of ours, seemed to be an exceptional choice, with a finished block comprised of nothing but squares. With the convenience of a block exchange and by strip piecing rather than cutting individual squares, we can sew and assemble a wide variety of blocks in a relatively short time. Specific pressing instructions make the quilt-top assembly go smoothly, even if you're setting the blocks side by side.

42-Cents Forever Stamp

By Jean Johnson; machine quilted by Sheri Mecom

Finished Quilt: 74" x 92½"
Finished Block: 13" x 13"

*Inspired by the United States Postal Service Forever stamps,
Jean created alternate blocks using leftover sashing strips.
Jean's gorgeous quilt has thousands of 1" squares!*

Materials

Yardage is based on 42"-wide fabric.

6 yards *total* of at least 36 assorted prints for blocks and sashing

3¾ yards of double-pink print for blocks, sashing, and setting triangles

⅛ yard of red solid for block centers

¾ yard of dark red print for binding

7½ yards of fabric for backing

82" x 101" piece of batting

Cutting

From the assorted prints, cut a *total* of:

126 strips, 1½" x 42"

From the double-pink print, cut:

4 squares, 20" x 20"; cut each square into quarters diagonally to yield 16 side setting triangles (you'll use 14 and have 2 left over)*

2 squares, 10½" x 10½"; cut each square in half diagonally to yield 4 corner triangles*

8 strips, 6½" x 42"; crosscut into 48 squares, 6½" x 6½"

14 strips, 1½" x 42"; crosscut into 80 strips, 1½" x 6½"

From the red solid, cut:

2 strips, 1½" x 42"; crosscut into 32 squares, 1½" x 1½"

From the dark red print, cut:

9 strips, 2" x 42"

These triangles are cut oversized and will be trimmed after the quilt top is assembled.

Making the Sashed Postage Stamp Blocks

1. Sew together six different 1½" x 42" assorted print strips along the long edges to make a 6½"-wide strip set. Press the seam allowances in one direction. Repeat to make a total of 21 strip sets, with each strip set made from six different fabrics. Crosscut the strip sets into 528 segments, 1½" wide. Set aside 48 segments for the alternate blocks.

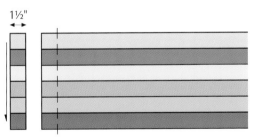

1½"

Make 21 strip sets.
Cut 528 segments.

2. Arrange six different segments into six horizontal rows as shown, rotating or re-pressing the segments so the seam allowances alternate direction from row to row. Join the segments to make a Postage Stamp block. The block should be 6½" square including the seam allowances. Press the seam allowances toward the bottom row. Repeat to make a total of 80 blocks.

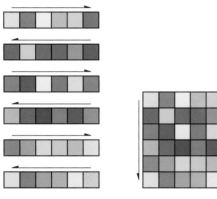

Make 80.

3. Lay out four Postage Stamp blocks, four 1½" x 6½" pink sashing strips, and one 1½" red square in three horizontal rows as shown. Sew the pieces in each row together. Press the seam allowances toward the sashing. Join the rows. Press the seam allowances toward the middle row. Repeat to make a total of 20 Sashed Postage Stamp blocks, each measuring 13½" square including the seam allowances.

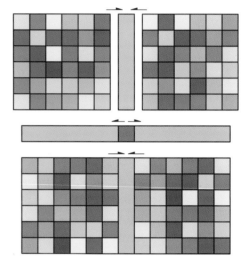

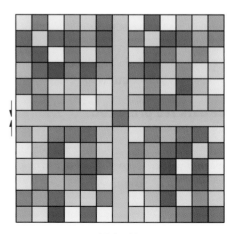

Make 20.

Making the Alternate Blocks

Lay out four 6½" pink squares, four strip-set segments set aside in step 1 of "Making the Sashed Postage Stamp Blocks," and one 1½" red square in three horizontal rows as shown. Sew the pieces in each row together. Press the seam allowances toward the pink and red squares. Join the rows. Press the seam allowances toward the top and bottom rows. Repeat to make a total of 12 alternate blocks, each measuring 13½" square including the seam allowances.

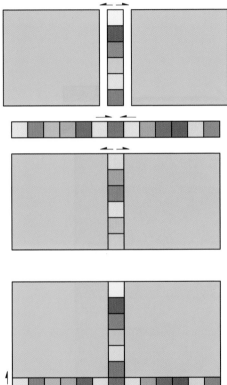

Make 12.

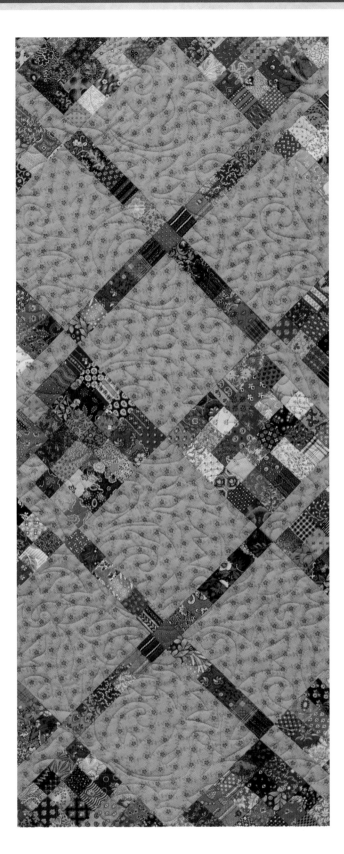

Assembling and Finishing the Quilt

For more details on quilting and finishing, go to ShopMartingale.com/HowtoQuilt.

1. Refer to the quilt assembly diagram below to arrange the blocks and pink side setting triangles in eight diagonal rows, alternating the blocks in each row and from row to row. Join the blocks and triangles in each row. Press the seam allowances toward the alternate blocks and side setting triangles. Join the rows. Press the seam allowances away from the center row. Add the corner triangles. Press the seam allowances toward the corner triangles.

2. Trim the quilt edges ¼" from the block points.

3. Cut and piece the backing so it's 4" larger than the quilt top on all sides. Layer the quilt top, batting, and backing; baste.

4. Quilt as desired. The quilt shown was machine quilted with a feather pattern.

5. Bind the quilt edges with the 2" x 42" pink strips.

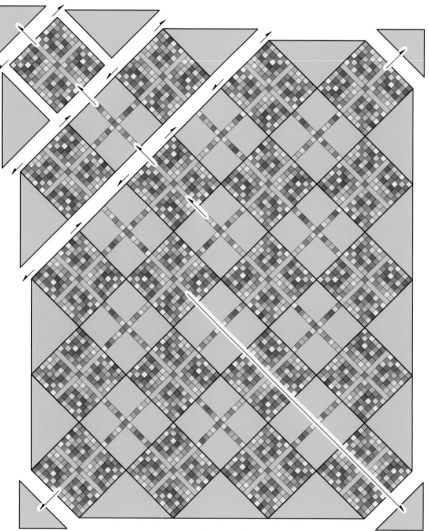

Quilt assembly

Pinwheels and Postage Stamps

By Peggy Morton; quilted by Lera Borden

FINISHED QUILT: 90½" x 108½"

Peggy alternated the Postage Stamp blocks with scrappy red 6"-finished Pinwheel blocks in a straight setting.

Zip Codes and Crossroads

By Janet Henderson; quilted by Sheri Mecom

FINISHED QUILT: 60" x 60"

Janet joined Postage Stamp blocks in groups of four to make larger 12"-finished blocks, and then separated the larger blocks with 1½"-wide sashing and cornerstones in a diagonal setting that includes pieced side and corner triangles.

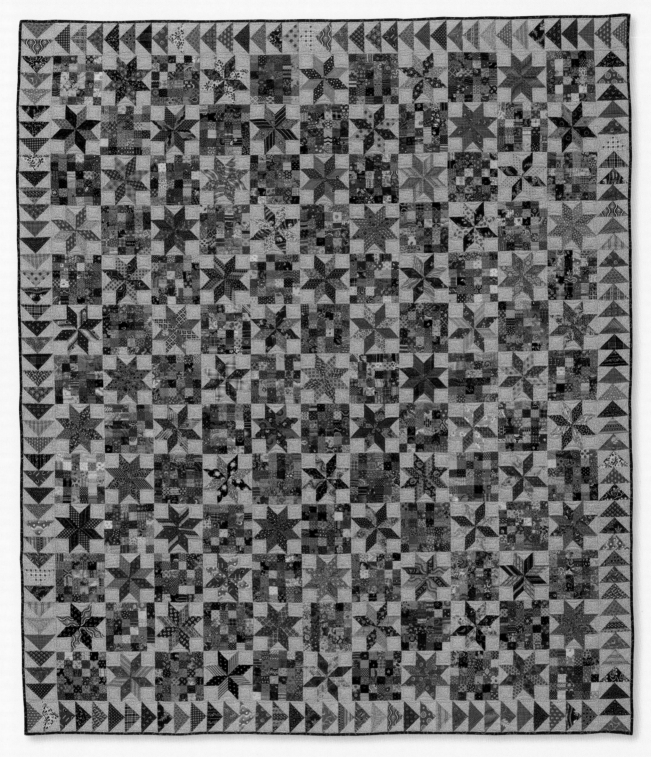

Postage Stamp and Lemoyne Stars

By Arlene Heintz; quilted by Julia Mason

Finished Quilt: 74½" x 86½"

Arlene alternated 6"-finished Lemoyne Star blocks with her Postage Stamp blocks and used 2" x 4" flying-geese units to create a border.

In all of our exchanges, we'd never considered a Pine Tree block until a scrappy version was proposed at a recent retreat. Inspired by an antique quilt seen at a Dallas quilt show, Deb Otto showed us an easy-to-piece tree trunk, and we were in! With units based on a 1" grid and pieced in quadrants, the blocks came together effortlessly.

Night and Day

By Deb Otto; quilted by Dawn Smith

FINISHED QUILT: 57" x 68⅜"
FINISHED BLOCK: 8" x 8"

In the featured quilt, Deb chose an unusual horizontal strip setting using prints in one of our favorite color combinations, indigo and cheddar, for the background. Bands of color frame the trees while allowing each pieced block to stand on its own merit.

Materials

Yardage is based on 42"-wide fabric. Fat eighths measure approximately 9" x 21".

1 fat eighth *each* of 30 assorted light shirting prints for Pine Tree block backgrounds

2 yards *total* of assorted medium and dark prints for Pine Tree block leaves

1⅞ yards of indigo print for setting pieces and binding

⅞ yard of cheddar print for setting pieces

5" x 6" rectangle *each* of 30 assorted brown prints for Pine Tree block trunks

3¾ yards of fabric for backing

65" x 77" piece of batting

Cutting

From *each* of the 30 assorted light shirting prints, cut:*

1 square, 4" x 4"; cut in half diagonally to yield 2 large A triangles (60 total)

1 square, 2⅞" x 2⅞"; cut in half diagonally to yield 2 medium B triangles (60 total; you'll use 30 and have 30 left over)

2 squares, 2½" x 2½" (60 total)

16 squares, 2" x 2" (480 total); cut each square in half diagonally to yield 32 small C triangles (960 total)

4 squares, 1½" x 1½" (120 total)

From the assorted medium and dark prints, cut a *total* of:

480 squares, 2" x 2"; cut each square in half diagonally to yield 960 small C triangles

90 squares, 1⅞" x 1⅞"; cut each square in half diagonally to yield 180 extra-small D triangles

From *each* of the 30 assorted brown prints, cut:**

1 square, 2⅞" x 2⅞"; cut in half diagonally to yield 2 medium B triangles (60 total; you'll use 30 and have 30 left over)

1 square, 2½" x 2½" (30 total)

2 squares, 1½" x 1½" (60 total)

From the cheddar print, cut:

8 squares, 9" x 9"

4 squares, 6⅝" x 6⅝"; cut each square in half diagonally to yield 8 small setting triangles

From the indigo print, cut:

7 strips, 2" x 42"

3 squares, 12⅝" x 12⅝"; cut each square into quarters diagonally to yield 12 large setting triangles (you'll use 10 and have 2 left over)

8 squares, 9" x 9"

4 squares, 8½" x 8½"

6 squares, 6⅝" x 6⅝"; cut each square in half diagonally to yield 12 small setting triangles

*Keep the pieces from each shirting print together.

**Keep the pieces from each brown print together.

Making the Pine Tree Blocks

The block is made up of four sections, each measuring 4½" square, including seam allowances. Measure these units as you go so that the finished block is accurate.

1. Select the pieces cut from one shirting print.

2. Carefully sew each shirting C triangle to a medium or dark C triangle along the long diagonal edges to make 32 half-square-triangle units. You are sewing bias edges together, so be careful not to stretch them. Press the seam allowances toward the medium or dark print. Square up each unit to 1½" x 1½".

Make 32.

3. Arrange 10 assorted half-square-triangle units from step 2 and three medium or dark D triangles into four horizontal rows. Sew the pieces in each row together. Press the seam allowances in alternating directions from row to row. Join the rows. Press the seam allowances toward the bottom row. Center and sew a shirting A triangle to the diagonal edge to complete the upper-left section. Press the seam allowances toward A, and then trim the A triangle even with the pieced half. The section should measure 4½" square, including seam allowances. Repeat to make the bottom right section, pressing the seam allowances of the joined rows toward the top row.

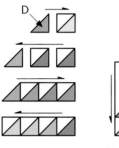

Upper left section.
Make 1.

Bottom right section.
Make 1.

4. Arrange the remaining 12 half-square-triangle units from step 2 and the four shirting print 1½" squares in four horizontal rows. Sew the pieces together in each row. Press the seam allowances in opposite directions from row to row. Join the rows to complete the upper-right section, which should measure 4½" square, including the seam

allowances. Press the seam allowances toward the bottom row.

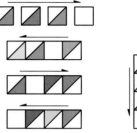

Upper right section.
Make 1.

5. To make the lower-left section, select the pieces cut from one brown print. Refer to step 2 to sew a shirting B triangle to a brown B triangle to make a half-square-triangle unit. Square up the unit to 2½" x 2½". Set aside the remaining shirting and brown triangles for another project.

6. Draw a diagonal line from corner to corner on the wrong side of each brown 1½" square. Layer a marked square on one corner of a 2½" shirting square. Sew on the marked line. Trim away the excess fabric ¼" from the stitching line. Press the seam allowances toward the brown print. Repeat to make a total of two units, each measuring 2½" square.

Make 2.

7. Arrange the units from steps 5 and 6 and the 2½" brown square into two horizontal rows. Sew the pieces in each row together. Press the seam allowances away from the units from step 6. Join the rows. Press the seam allowances toward the top row, the section should measure 4½" square, including the seam allowances.

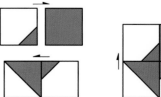

Lower left section.
Make 1.

8. Lay out the sections from steps 3, 4, and 7 into two horizontal rows as shown. Sew together the pieces in each row. Press the seam allowances as indicated. Join the rows. Press the seam allowances toward the bottom row. The block should measure 8½" square, including the seam allowances.

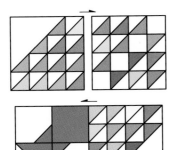

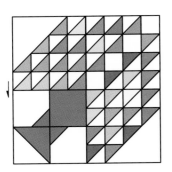

9. Repeat steps 1–8 to make a total of 30 blocks.

Making the Setting Pieces

1. Draw a diagonal line from corner to corner on the wrong side of each 9" cheddar square. Layer a marked square on top of a 9" indigo square, right sides together. Sew ¼" from each side of the marked line. Cut the squares apart on the marked line to make two setting blocks. Press the seam allowances toward the indigo piece. Repeat to make a total of 16 setting blocks. Square up each block to 8½" x 8½".

Make 16.

2. Join the indigo and cheddar small setting triangles along their short edges as shown to make a pieced setting triangle. Press the seam allowances toward the indigo triangles. Set aside the remaining four indigo small triangles for setting corners.

Make 4.   Make 4.

Assembling and Finishing the Quilt

For more details on quilting and finishing, go to ShopMartingale.com/HowtoQuilt.

1. Refer to the assembly diagram below to arrange the Pine Tree blocks, pieced setting blocks, pieced setting triangles, 8½" indigo setting squares, and large indigo side setting triangles into 10 diagonal rows as shown. Join the pieces in each row. Press the seam allowances toward the setting blocks and triangles. Join the rows. Press the seam allowances away from the center row. Add the remaining indigo small setting triangles to the corners. Press the seam allowances toward the corners.

2. Cut and piece the backing so it's 4" larger than the quilt top on all sides. Layer the quilt top, batting, and backing; baste.

3. Quilt as desired. The quilt shown was machine quilted in the ditch of the tree triangles. Feathered wreathes fill the alternate blocks.

4. Bind the quilt edges with the 2" x 42" indigo strips.

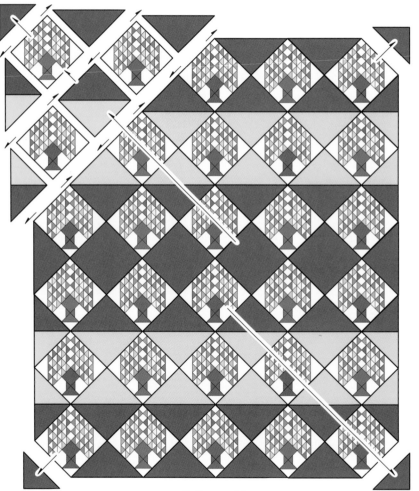

Quilt assembly

Trees of Swinney Switch

By Linda Cordell; machine quilted by Julia Mason

FINISHED QUILT: 70¼" x 83¾"

Linda added corner triangles to the Pine Tree blocks to make 11¼"-finished blocks. The blocks are set straight with 2¼"-wide pieced sashing strips.

23

Cabin Trees

By Ramona Williams; machine quilted by Melba Drennan

FINISHED QUILT: 57" x 68⅜"

Half light, half dark Log Cabin blocks with a 2" center four-patch unit alternate with the Pine Tree blocks in a diagonal setting reminiscent of mountains.

Almost Christmas Pines

By Stacey Barrington; machine quilted by Sandy Towey

FINISHED QUILT: 86" x 86"

Using only Pine Tree blocks, Stacey added 3"-wide sashing strips with 3"-finished nine-patch cornerstones between the blocks. The diagonal setting is framed with a 4"-wide border that features more nine-patch units in two of the corners.

The traditional Album block is also known as a Signature block when the center section is a light-colored solid fabric. After seeing the fabulous nearly queen-size antique quilt top that Deb Otto had purchased, made in Pennsylvania circa 1880 (shown on page 35), we were inspired to reproduce this fabric-lover's delight. The scrappy blocks were rather small at 4" square, and there were 289 of them, each containing wonderful old fabrics. To make rotary cutting and piecing easier, we enlarged the block just a bit.

The Arlington Album Quilt

By Annette Plog; machine quilted by Sheri Mecom

FINISHED QUILT: 60⅞" x 77¾"
FINISHED BLOCK: 5" x 5"

Annette set the blocks against indigo, one of her favorite colors. Sashing, cornerstones, setting triangles, and the outer border are all the same indigo print, which helps make the colorful Album blocks appear to float.

Materials

Yardage is based on 42"-wide fabric.

3¾ yards of indigo print for sashing, setting triangles, border, and binding

2¼ yards *total* of assorted light and medium prints (lights) for block backgrounds

2¼ yards *total* of assorted medium and dark prints (darks) for blocks

5¼ yards of fabric for backing

69" x 86" piece of batting

Cutting

CUTTING FOR BLOCKS

The cutting instructions are for one block. For each block, select one light or medium print for the center and outer pieces and select a contrasting medium or dark print for the middle "ring." To add variety to the blocks, use two medium or dark prints for the middle ring, cutting rectangles from one print and squares from the other. Repeat the instructions to cut pieces for 83 blocks. Keep the pieces for each block together.

From the darks, cut:

4 rectangles, 1⅜" x 3⅛"

8 squares, 1⅜" x 1⅜"

From the lights, cut:

3 squares, 2½" x 2½"; cut each square into quarters diagonally to yield 12 side triangles

2 squares, 1½" x 1½"; cut each square in half diagonally to yield 4 corner triangles

1 rectangle, 1⅜" x 3⅛"

2 squares, 1⅜" x 1⅜"

CUTTING FOR REMAINING PIECES

From the indigo print, cut:

2 strips, 9¾" x 42"; crosscut into 6 squares, 9¾" x 9¾". Cut each square into quarters diagonally to yield 24 side setting triangles.

7 strips, 4½" x 42"

8 strips, 2" x 42"

2 squares, 5⅞" x 5⅞"; cut each square in half diagonally to yield 4 corner setting triangles

32 strips, 1½" x 5½"; crosscut into:

192 rectangles, 1½" x 5½"

110 squares, 1½" x 1½"

Making the Album Blocks

1. Select the pieces cut for one block.

2. Sew 1⅜" dark squares to opposite sides of a 1⅜" light square. Press the seam allowances toward the dark squares. Repeat to make a total of two 1⅜" x 3⅛" units.

Make 2.

3. Join a unit from step 1 to each long edge of the 1⅜" x 3⅛" light rectangle. Press the seam allowances toward the rectangle. This unit should measure 3⅛" square, including seam allowances.

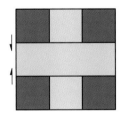

4. Sew 1⅜" x 3⅛" dark rectangles to the sides of the unit from step 3. Press the seam allowances toward the newly added rectangles.

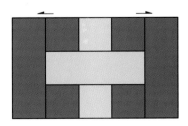

5. Sew a light side triangle to the ends of a 1⅜" x 3⅛" dark rectangle. Press the seam allowances toward the triangles. Repeat to make a total of two units. Sew these units to the top and bottom of the unit from step 4. Press the seam allowances toward the newly added rectangle units.

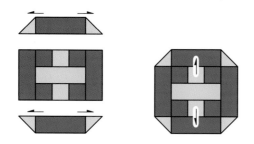

6. Sew light side triangles to opposite sides of each of the remaining four 1⅜" dark squares. Press the seam allowances toward the triangles. Add a light or medium corner triangle to the top of each unit. Press the seam allowances toward the corner triangle.

Make 4.

7. Sew corner units from step 6 to opposite sides of the unit from step 5. Press the seam allowances toward the corner units. Repeat with the remaining corners. Square up the block to 5½" x 5½".

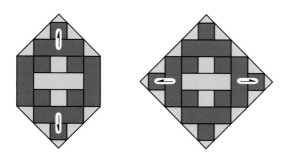

8. Repeat steps 1–7 to make a total of 83 blocks.

Assembling and Finishing the Quilt

For more details on quilting and finishing, go to ShopMartingale.com/HowtoQuilt.

1. Refer to the quilt assembly diagram on page 31 to arrange the blocks, 1½" x 5½" indigo sashing rectangles, 1½" indigo sashing squares, and indigo side setting triangles in diagonal rows. Join the blocks and sashing rectangles in each block row. Join the sashing rectangles and cornerstones in each sashing row. Press the seam allowances toward the sashing strips.

2. Referring to the quilt assembly diagram, join a sashing row to the top or bottom of each block row. Press the seam allowances toward the sashing row. Add the side setting triangles to the ends of the appropriate rows. Press the seam allowances toward the setting triangles. Join the rows. Press the seam allowances away from the center row. Add the indigo corner setting triangles. Press the seam allowances toward the corner triangles.

Why Use Matching Cornerstones?

Annette used cornerstones cut from the sashing fabric to make the quilt assembly easier. We've often referred to them as "faux stones" because they aren't noticed; they match the sashing fabric and give the illusion of continuous sashing. However, the seamlines make it very easy to align the blocks accurately from row to row without tedious pin-matching across the sashing strips.

3. Join the 4½" x 42" indigo strips end to end to make one long strip. Press the seam allowances in one direction. Measure the quilt top through the center from top to bottom. From the pieced strip, cut two strips the length measured. Sew

these strips to the sides of the quilt top. Press the seam allowances toward the strips. Measure the quilt top through the center from side to side, including the border strips. From the remainder of the pieced strip, cut two strips to the length measured. Sew these strips to the top and bottom of the quilt top. Press the seam allowances toward the strips.

4. Cut and piece the backing so it's 4" larger than the quilt top on all sides. Layer the quilt top, batting, and backing; baste.

5. Quilt as desired. The quilt shown was machine quilted with a Baptist Fan pattern.

6. Bind the quilt edges with the 2" x 42" indigo strips.

Quilt assembly

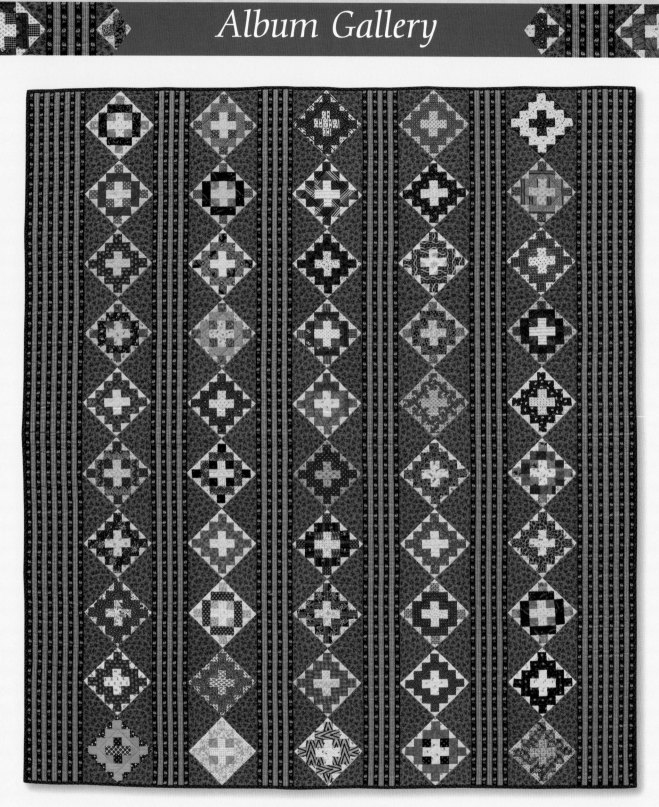

It's a Sweep

By Betty Edgell; machine quilted by Sheri Mecom

FINISHED QUILT: 61" x 70½"

Betty set blocks on point in vertical rows separated by boldly striped 3½"-wide strips. Side borders measure 5¾" wide.

Album Redux

By Deb Otto; machine quilted by Dawn Smith

FINISHED QUILT: 64½" x 89½"

Deb used 1"-wide sashing between the four-block sections.
The indigo sashing and pink cornerstones are 1½" wide.

Album Baskets

By Mary Freeman; machine quilted by Gail Rowland

Finished Quilt: 73½" x 84⅝"

The sashing and cornerstones are 1" wide, and the Basket blocks used in the borders are 5"-finished. The bottom border includes four 1⅛"-wide spacer strips to fit the quilt width.

Antique Album Quilt

Owned by Deb Otto

FINISHED QUILT TOP: 86½" x 86½"

The Divas were awed by this antique quilt make of 289 blocks, just 4" square each. While it's comprised of dozens of fabrics, notice how the solid cheddar is grouped in the center of the quilt.

35

O nce again the Patchwork Divas took inspiration for an exchange from a great and somewhat challenging block, Wild Goose Chase. Having seen a number of antique quilts with the block over the years, the group expanded its options to give each Diva a choice—a scrappy block of multiple colors or an Americana version using reds, shirting prints, and blues. The resulting blocks in both options were stunning.

Chasing a Wild Diva

Made and hand quilted by Diana Petterson

FINISHED QUILT: 81⅞" x 98⅛"
FINISHED BLOCK: 11½" x 11½"

Diana set the scrappy blocks she received in the exchange on point and alternated them with plain setting squares. She finished her quilt with beautiful hand quilting using pearl cotton and a Baptist Fan design.

Materials

Yardage is based on 42"-wide fabric. Fat eighths measure approximately 9" x 21".

2⅓ yards *total* of assorted light prints *OR* 30 fat eighths for blocks

2⅓ yards *total* of assorted dark prints *OR* 30 fat eighths for blocks

4⅛ yards of tan print for setting squares and triangles

⅔ yard of dark red print for binding

7½ yards of fabric for backing

90" x 107" piece of batting

Cutting

CUTTING FOR BLOCKS

The cutting instructions are for one block. For each block, select one of the assorted light prints and two of the assorted dark prints (one for the A squares and one for the B triangles). To add variety to the blocks, three dark prints (one each for the A, B, and C pieces) or an assortment of dark prints were occasionally used for the B triangles. Repeat the instructions to cut pieces for 30 blocks. Keep the pieces for each block together.

From 1 of the dark prints, cut:

5 squares, 2⅞" x 2⅞" (A)

2 squares, 4⅝" x 4⅝"; cut each square into quarters diagonally to yield 8 triangles (B)*

From the remaining dark print, cut:

1 square, 8⅜" x 8⅜"; cut into quarters diagonally to yield 4 triangles (C)*

From 1 of the light prints, cut:

14 squares, 2⅝" x 2⅝"; cut each square in half diagonally to yield 28 triangles (D)*

These triangles are cut oversized and will be trimmed as the blocks are constructed.

CUTTING FOR REMAINING PIECES

From the tan print, cut:

3 strips, 17⅝" x 42"; crosscut into 5 squares, 17⅝" x 17⅝". Cut each square into quarters diagonally to yield 20 side setting triangles (you'll use 18 and have 2 left over).**

7 strips, 12" x 42"; crosscut into 20 squares, 12" x 12"

2 squares, 9¼" x 9¼"; cut each square in half diagonally to yield 4 corner triangles**

From the dark red print, cut:

10 strips, 2" x 42"

**These triangles are cut oversized and will be trimmed as the quilt top is assembled.

Making the Wild Goose Chase Blocks

1. Select the pieces cut for one block.

2. Sew D triangles to opposite sides of an A square. Press the seam allowances toward the triangles. Sew D triangles to the remaining two sides of the square to make the block center unit. Press the seam allowances toward the square. Square up the unit to 3¾" x 3¾".

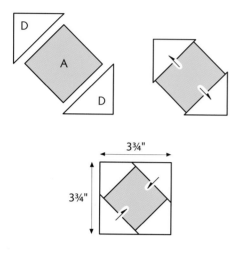

3. Sew D triangles to both short sides of a B triangle to make a flying-geese unit. Press the seam allowances toward the D triangles. Repeat to make a total of eight flying-geese units. Trim each unit to 2⅛" x 3¾".

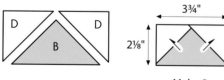

Make 8.

4. Join two flying-geese units along the long edges as shown. Press the seam allowances toward the top unit. Repeat to make a total of four pairs.

Make 4.

5. Sew D triangles to two adjacent sides of an A square. Press the seam allowances toward the triangles. Trim the unit so the long straight edge measures 2¾", and then trim the long edge ¼" from the point of the square. Repeat to make a total of four units.

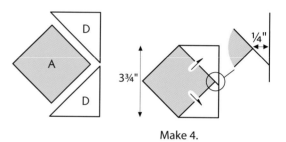

Make 4.

6. Join a flying-geese pair to a unit from step 5. Press the seam allowances toward the flying geese. Repeat to make a total of four units.

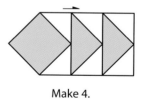

Make 4.

7. Sew two units from step 6 to opposite sides of the center unit from step 2 to make the block center section. Press the seam allowances toward the center unit.

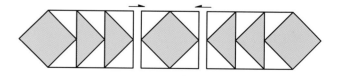

9. Join the corner sections to the long edges of the center section to complete the block. Press the seam allowances toward the corner sections. Square up the block to 12" x 12".

8. Join two C triangles to opposite long edges of a unit from step 6. Press the seam allowances toward the triangles. Repeat to make a total of two corner sections.

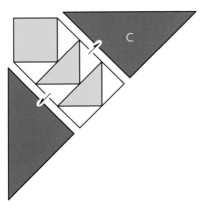

Make 2.

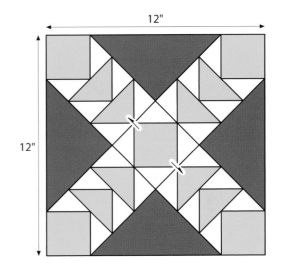

12"

12"

10. Repeat steps 1–9 to make a total of 30 blocks.

Assembling and Finishing the Quilt

For more details on quilting and finishing, go to ShopMartingale.com/HowtoQuilt.

1. Refer to the quilt assembly diagram below to arrange the blocks, tan print squares, and light side setting triangles in 10 diagonal rows, alternating the blocks in each row and from row to row. Join the blocks and triangles in each row. Press the seam allowances toward the tan squares and side setting triangles. Join the rows. Press the seam allowances away from the center row. Add the light corner triangles. Press the seam allowances toward the corner triangles.

2. Trim the quilt edges ¼" from the block points.

3. Cut and piece the backing so it's 4" larger than the quilt top on all sides. Layer the quilt top, batting, and backing; baste.

4. Quilt as desired. The quilt show was hand quilted in the Baptist Fan pattern.

5. Bind the quilt edges with the 2" x 42" dark red strips.

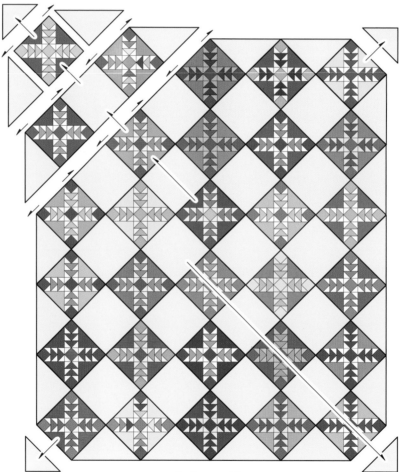

Quilt assembly

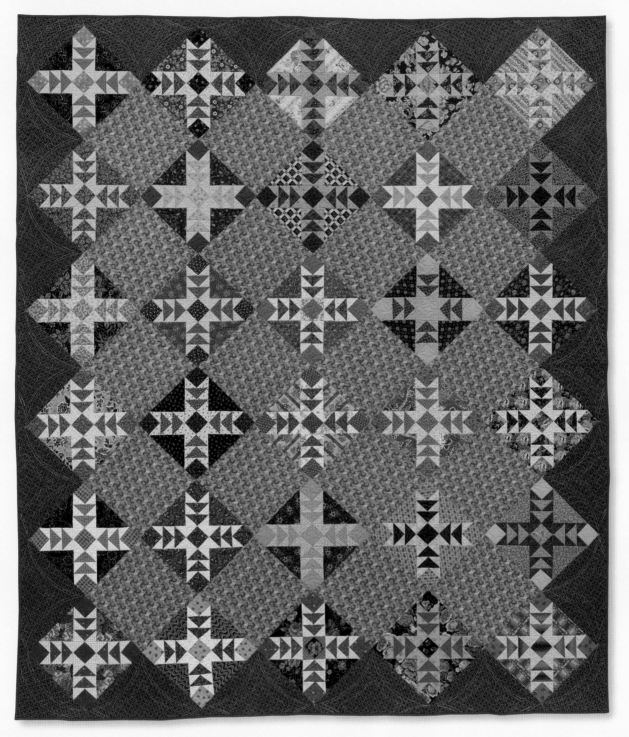

Chasing Geese Again

By Karen Roxburgh; machine quilted by Rita Meyerhoff

FINISHED QUILT: 81⅞" x 98⅛"

Karen's quilt is set the same as the featured quilt, but rather than using matching fabrics for her alternate squares and setting triangles, she chose two different prints.

43

Wild Goose Chase

By Sue Troyan; machine quilted by Sheri Mecom

Finished Quilt: 105½" x 105½"

Sue set blocks in straight rows with alternate cheddar print squares. This quilt is framed with a 1"-wide red inner border and a 6"-wide cheddar outer border.

Freedom

By Betsy Chutchian; machine quilted by Sheri Mecom

FINISHED QUILT: 58" x 69½"

Betsy used 30 patriotic blocks set side by side in a straight setting of six rows of five blocks each, with no sashing or alternate blocks.

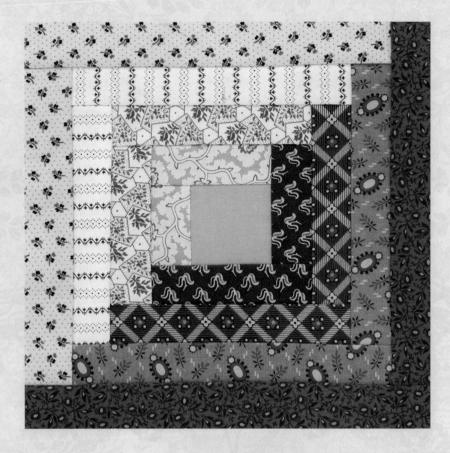

A timeless, best-loved block, the Log Cabin was one we had long wanted to exchange. Julia Berggren's antique summer bedspread, shown on page 55, provided the inspiration. After choosing the finished size of the logs and center square, we offered members the choice of using a traditional red or cheddar center. For continuity when the blocks were exchanged, everyone used the same red or cheddar fabric to make the blocks according to each Patchwork Diva's choice.

Point of No Return

By Carol Staehle; machine quilted by Sheri Mecom

FINISHED QUILT: 60½" x 68"
FINISHED BLOCK: 7½" x 7½"

*Inspired by the Chevron setting of a late 1800s quilt
(a modified Straight Furrows setting), Carol decided to let the
graphic block arrangement stand alone without a border.*

Materials

Yardage is based on 42"-wide fabric.

3⅓ yards *total* of assorted dark prints for blocks

3 yards *total* of assorted light prints for blocks

⅓ yard of Turkey red *OR* cheddar solid for block centers

½ yard of dark print for binding

4¼ yards of fabric for backing

69" x 76" piece of batting

Cutting

CUTTING FOR LOGS

The cutting instructions are for one block. For each block, select four light prints and four dark prints. Repeat the instructions to cut logs for 72 blocks. Label the pieces with the letter given and keep the pieces for each block together in alphabetical order for ease in piecing the blocks.

Note: *Whenever possible, cut the pieces for the logs along the lengthwise grain of your fabric. Your blocks will be more accurate and lie flatter.*

From light #1, cut:

1 rectangle, 1¼" x 2" (A)

1 rectangle, 1¼" x 2¾" (B)

From dark #1, cut:

1 rectangle, 1¼" x 2¾" (C)

1 rectangle, 1¼" x 3½" (D)

From light #2, cut:

1 rectangle, 1¼" x 3½" (E)

1 rectangle, 1¼" x 4¼" (F)

From dark #2, cut:

1 rectangle, 1¼" x 4¼" (G)

1 rectangle, 1¼" x 5" (H)

From light #3, cut:

1 rectangle, 1¼" x 5" (I)

1 rectangle, 1¼" x 5¾" (J)

From dark #3, cut:

1 rectangle, 1¼" x 5¾" (K)

1 rectangle, 1¼" x 6½" (L)

From light #4, cut:

1 rectangle, 1¼" x 6½" (M)

1 rectangle, 1¼" x 7¼" (N)

From dark #4, cut:

1 rectangle, 1¼" x 7¼" (O)

1 rectangle, 1¼" x 8" (P)

Log-Cutting Tip

To accommodate sewing differences for block-exchange groups, you may wish to increase the width of the logs in the outer round (logs M–P) to 1⅜" or even 1½". Any excess can be trimmed when squaring up the blocks.

CUTTING FOR REMAINING PIECES

From the Turkey red or cheddar solid, cut:

4 strips, 2" x 42"; crosscut into 72 squares, 2" x 2"

From the dark print for binding, cut:

7 strips, 2" x 42"

Making the Log Cabin Blocks

Press all seam allowances toward the newly added log in each step.

1. Select the logs for one block. Sew log A to the left edge of a red or cheddar square; press. Add log B to the top edge of this unit; press.

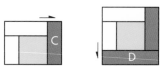

2. Sew log C to the right edge of the unit from step 1; press. Add log D to the bottom edge of this unit; press. The unit should measure 3½" x 3½" after the first round of logs has been attached.

It Takes Two Seams

After round 1 is complete, always add the next log to the side of the block that has two seams.

3. Add logs E–P in the same manner, working clockwise around the center square in alphabetical order. The unit should measure 5" x 5" after round 2; it should measure 6½" x 6½" after round 3. After the round 4 logs are joined, square up the block to 8" x 8".

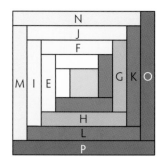

4. Repeat steps 1–3 to make a total of 72 blocks.

Assembling and Finishing the Quilt

For more details on quilting and finishing, go to ShopMartingale.com/HowtoQuilt.

1. Refer to the quilt assembly diagram below to arrange the blocks in nine rows of eight blocks each. Sew the blocks in each row together. Press the seam allowances in alternating directions from row to row. Join the rows. Press the seam allowances in one direction.

2. Cut and piece the backing so it's 4" larger than the quilt top on all sides. Layer the quilt top, batting, and backing; baste.

3. Quilt as desired. The quilt shown was machine quilted in an allover Baptist Fan pattern.

4. Bind the quilt edges with the 2" x 42" dark strips.

Quilt assembly

Zigzag Log Cabin

By Marilyn Mowry; machine quilted by Sheri Mecom

FINISHED QUILT: 60½" x 75½"

Marilyn rotated the blocks she received in the exchange to create horizontal zigzag rows (Streak of Lightning setting) alternating with rows of on-point squares (Sunshine and Shadow setting).

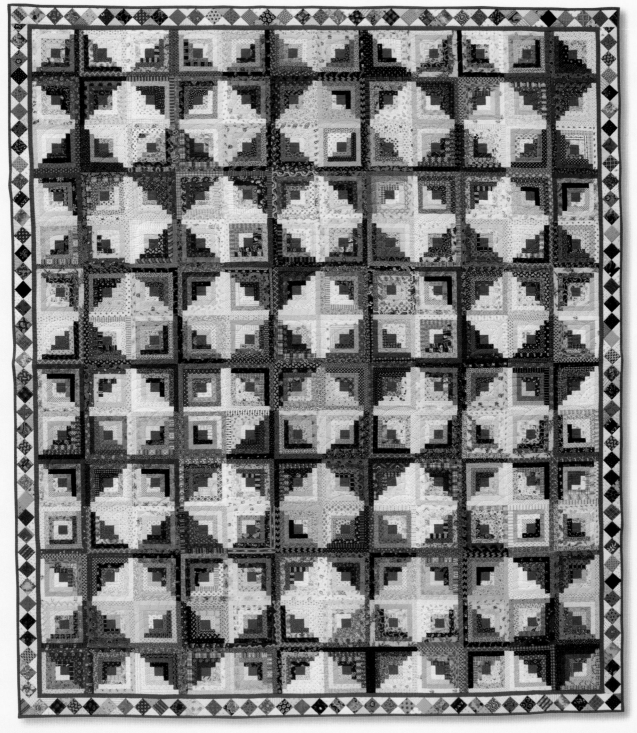

Cabin Squares

By Peggy Morton; machine quilted by Linda Carlson

FINISHED QUILT: 97" x 112"

Using 168 blocks, Peggy created a Sunshine and Shadow setting and framed it with a ¾"-wide red inner border and a 2¾"-wide square-in-a-square outer border.

Susan's Cabin

By Julia Berggren; machine quilted by Sheri Mecom

FINISHED QUILT: 75½" x 75½"

Julia created a traditional Barn Raising setting with 100 blocks set side by side.

Antique Summer Spread

Owned by Julia Berggren

FINISHED QUILT: 72½" x 72½"

*A unique variation of the Barn Raising setting
is found in this stunning antique quilt.*

Do you love indigo fabric like *we* love indigo fabric? How about Basket blocks? The Patchwork Divas love both, so combining the two in one block was easy and inspiring. Adding a cheddar print to the mix gave us even more to love.

Somerset Baskets

By Marilyn Mowry; machine quilted by Sheri Mecom

FINISHED QUILT: 53½" x 53½"
FINISHED BASKET BLOCK: 7½" x 7½"

Marilyn's husband was a willing helper when it was time to set her Basket blocks. Together they played with various layouts and settled on the blocks coming together in quadrants. Don't you love the secondary pattern made by this arrangement?

Materials

Yardage is based on 42"-wide fabric.

⅝ yards *total* of assorted cheddar prints for blocks (cheddar #1)

1½ yards of cheddar print for sashing, border, and binding (cheddar #2)

1⅔ yards *total* of assorted indigo prints for blocks

1⅞ yards of cream solid for blocks

3½ yards of fabric for backing

62" x 62" piece of batting

Cutting

CUTTING FOR BLOCKS

The cutting instructions are for the indigo and cheddar pieces for one block. Cutting instructions for the cream background pieces are given in "Cutting for Remaining Pieces." For each block, select one indigo print and one print from the assorted cheddars (cheddar #1). Repeat the instructions to cut the pieces for 36 blocks. Keep the pieces for each block together.

From cheddar #1, cut:

3 squares, 2½" x 2½"

From the indigo print, cut:

7 squares, 2½" x 2½"

2 squares, 2⅜" x 2⅜"; cut in half diagonally to yield 4 triangles

CUTTING FOR REMAINING PIECES

From the cream solid, cut:

4 strips, 3⅞" x 42"; crosscut into 36 squares, 3⅞" x 3⅞". Cut each square in half diagonally to yield 72 triangles.

9 strips, 2½" x 42"; crosscut into 144 squares, 2½" x 2½"

9 strips, 2" x 42"; crosscut into 72 rectangles, 2" x 5"

From cheddar #2, cut:

6 strips, 3¼" x 42"

6 strips, 2" x 42"

12 strips, 1" x 42"; crosscut *6 of the strips* into 30 strips, 1" x 8"

Making the Indigo Basket Blocks

1. Draw a diagonal line from corner to corner on the wrong side of each 2½" cream square. Repeat with the cheddar #1 squares in each of the 36 sets of block pieces.

2. Select the cheddar and indigo pieces to use for one block.

3. Layer a marked cheddar square on top of a 2½" indigo square, right sides together. Sew ¼" from each side of the marked line. Cut the squares apart on the marked line to make two half-square-triangle units. Press the seam allowances toward the indigo triangles. Repeat to make a total of six cheddar half-square-triangle units. Square up each unit to 2" x 2".

Make 6.

4. Repeat step 3 with four marked cream squares and the remaining four indigo 2½" squares to make eight cream half-square-triangle units. You will use seven units and have one left over.

Make 8.

5. Sew indigo triangles to the cheddar sides of a cheddar half-square-triangle unit. Press the seam allowances toward the indigo triangles.

6. Sew a cream triangle to the diagonal edge of the unit from step 5. Square up the unit to 3½" x 3½".

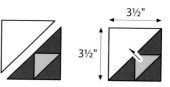

7. Sew two cheddar half-square-triangle units together as shown. Press the seam allowances toward the bottom unit. Join this unit to the right edge of the unit from step 6. Press the seam allowances toward the unit from step 6.

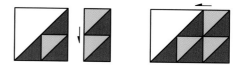

8. Join the remaining three cheddar half-square-triangle units side by side. Press the seam allowances toward the right. Add this unit to the bottom of the unit from step 7. Press the seam allowances toward the bottom row. The unit should measure 5" x 5", including the seam allowances.

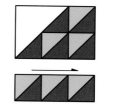

9. Join the cream half-square-triangle units into one horizontal three-unit row and one vertical four-unit row. Press the seam allowances as indicated.

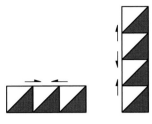

Make 1 of each.

10. Add the three-unit row from step 9 to the top of the unit from step 8. Press the seam allowances toward the bottom of the unit. Join the four-unit row from step 9 to the left edge of the unit. Press the seam allowances toward the center of the unit.

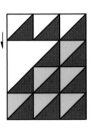 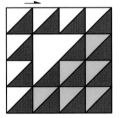

11. Sew the remaining indigo triangles to the ends of two 2" x 5" cream rectangles as shown. Press the seam allowances as indicated.

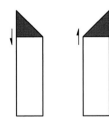

12. Join the units from step 11 to the right and bottom edges of the unit from step 10. Press the seam allowances as indicated. Add a cream triangle to the bottom-right corner. Press the seam allowances toward the triangle. The block should measure 8" x 8", including the seam allowances.

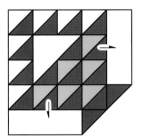

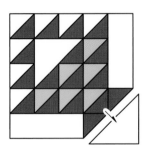

13. Repeat steps 1–12 to make a total of 36 Indigo Basket blocks.

Assembling and Finishing the Quilt

For more details on quilting and finishing, go to ShopMartingale.com/HowtoQuilt.

1. Using cheddar #2, alternately arrange six blocks and five cheddar 1" x 8" sashing strips in one horizontal row, rotating the blocks as shown. Sew the pieces together. Press the seam allowances toward the sashing. Repeat to make a total of six rows.

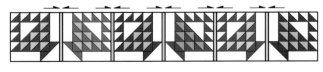

Make 6.

2. Join the remaining six 1" x 42" cheddar strips end to end to make one long strip. From the pieced strip, cut five sashing strips, 1" x 48".

3. Refer to the quilt assembly diagram below to arrange the block rows and sashing strips, rotating the rows as shown to create the pattern. Sew the rows and strips together. Press the seam allowances toward the sashing rows.

4. Join the 3¼" x 42" cheddar strips end to end to make one long strip. From the pieced strip, cut two border strips, 48" long. Sew these strips to the sides of the quilt top. Press the seam allowances

toward the borders. From the remainder of the pieced strip, cut two border strips, 53½" long. Sew these strips to the top and bottom of the quilt top. Press the seam allowances toward the borders.

5. Cut and piece the backing so it's 4" larger than the quilt top on all sides. Layer the quilt top, batting, and backing; baste.

6. Quilt as desired. The quilt shown was machine quilted in grids of parallel diagonal lines that play off the angles in the blocks.

7. Bind the quilt edges with the 2" x 42" cheddar strips.

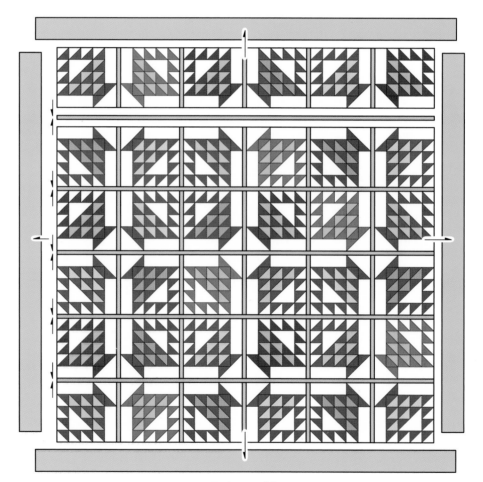

Quilt assembly

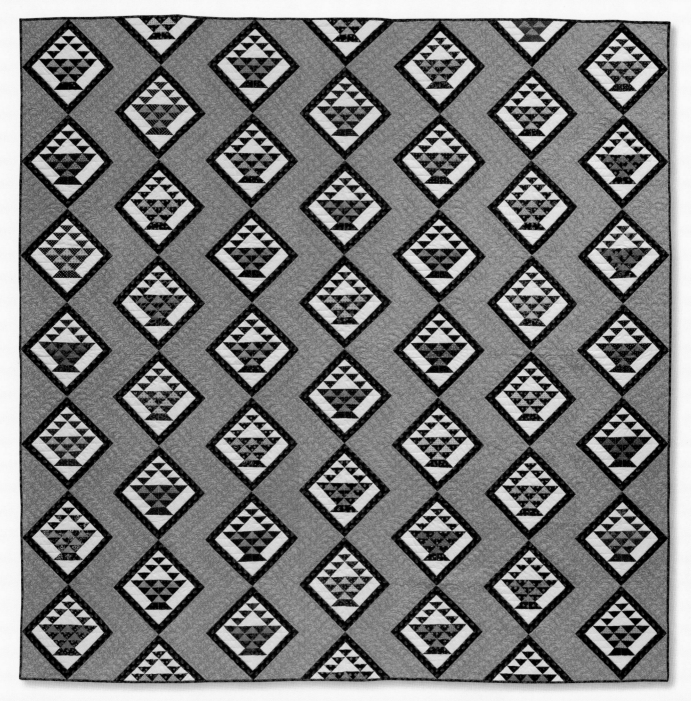

Baskets in a Field of Coreopsis

By Janet Henderson; machine quilted by Sheri Mecom

FINISHED QUILT: 94½" x 94½"

Janet framed the blocks with 1"-finished indigo print strips and then arranged them with cheddar setting triangles to create vertical strips that are 13½"-wide finished. She used half blocks at the top and bottom of alternate strips to offset the blocks, creating a zigzag setting.

Don't Fence Me In

By Carol Staehle; machine quilted by Sheri Mecom

Finished Quilt: 63½" x 74⅛"

Carol set Basket blocks on point with 7½"-finished setting squares and framed them with a 5"-wide zigzag border. Notice how the border pattern doesn't meet in the corners, in true-to-the-past style, which adds a bit of whimsy to an otherwise formal quilt.

Stacked Baskets

By Betsy Chutchian; machine quilted by Sheri Mecom

FINISHED QUILT: 57¾" x 77"

Betsy used a zigzag setting and cut the setting triangles from a striped fabric. She alternated the direction of the stripes, which creates lots of movement in the design. The quilt was assembled in three vertical panels.

A s a challenge for the group, Betsy and Carol suggested a foundation-pieced Sunburst block and a template-based Sunflower block (see page 100). Each Diva could then choose which one she wanted to make, and several decided to make both! Both methods were quite a departure from the usual routine of strip piecing and assembly sewing, though some Divas did assembly line sew the units. The resulting blocks of both exchanges were stunning, and setting inspirations were gleaned from the beautiful quilts of the early 1800s.

Daybreak

By Betsy Chutchian; machine quilted by Sheri Mecom

FINISHED QUILT: 64⅛" x 85⅜"
FINISHED BLOCK: 15" x 15"

Betsy was drawn to a simple cream fabric for the block background that contrasted beautifully with the chintz fabrics used for the sunburst appliqués. To set the blocks, she found inspiration in the pieced diamond border of an antique quilt and translated it to a frame around each block, which appeared as sashing in the finished quilt. Taking things a step further, she made half and quarter blocks for the setting triangles, making this quilt look more complicated than it actually is.

Materials

Yardage is based on 42"-wide fabric.

4½" x 42" strip *each* of 24 assorted prints for block spikes

⅜ yard *each* of 24 coordinating prints for block triangles and centers

5⅝ yards of cream solid for block backgrounds and pieced frames

2⅛ yards of brown floral for pieced frames

⅝ yard of brown print for binding

5¾ yards of fabric for backing

72" x 94" piece of batting

Template plastic

Foundation-piecing paper

Cutting

Before you begin cutting, trace the spike and triangle patterns on page 73 onto template plastic and cut them out. Use the templates to cut the pieces from the fabrics indicated.

From *each of 18* of the assorted prints, cut:

16 spike pieces (group #1)

From *each of 5* of the remaining assorted prints, cut:

18 spike pieces (group #2)

From the remaining assorted print, cut:

20 spike pieces (group #3)

From *each of 18* of the coordinating prints, cut:

16 triangle pieces (group #1)

1 square, 5" x 5"

From *each of 5* of the remaining coordinating prints, cut:

18 triangle pieces (group #2)

2 squares, 5" x 5"

From the remaining coordinating print, cut:

16 triangle pieces (group #3)

4 squares, 5" x 5"

From the cream solid, cut:

2 strips, 18¾" x 42"; crosscut into 3 squares, 18¾" x 18¾". Cut each square into quarters diagonally to yield 12 side setting triangles (you'll use 10 and have 2 left over).

6 strips, 13" x 42"; crosscut into 18 squares, 13" x 13"

28 strips, 2⅜" x 42"; crosscut into 439 squares, 2⅜" x 2⅜"*

2 squares, 9⅜" x 9⅜"; cut each square in half diagonally to yield 4 corner setting triangles

From the brown floral, cut:

28 strips, 2⅜" x 42"; crosscut into 439 squares, 2⅜" x 2⅜"*

From the brown print, cut:

8 strips, 2" x 42"

*Before cutting the cream and brown 2⅜" squares, consider using preprinted papers created specifically for making half-square-triangle units. These papers can speed up the process and increase the accuracy of making your half-square-triangle units. For the block frames, look for papers that make 1½" finished units. Purchase enough papers to make 878 half-square-triangle units and follow the instructions provided with the papers to make the units.

Preparing the Paper Foundations

1. Photocopy or trace the patterns on pages 74–76 onto foundation paper. Make 18 *each* of patterns A and B, 5 *each* of patterns C and D, and 4 of pattern E. Trim any excess paper around each foundation-paper piece, leaving approximately ½" beyond the dashed outer lines of the patterns.

2. Fold and crease each pattern along the straight solid lines of the spike and triangle shapes (not the solid inner and outer curved lines) to mark the stitching lines.

Paper Piecing the Sunburst Appliqués

If you need more information on paper piecing, go to ShopMartingale.com/HowtoQuilt for free downloadable instructions.

1. Pair 16 matching group #1 spike pieces with 16 coordinating group #1 triangle pieces to make a set. Repeat for the remaining group #1 pieces to make a total of 18 sets. In the same manner, make 5 sets of group #2 pieces and 1 set of group #3 pieces.

2. Select one set of group #1 pieces. Paper piece one A pattern and one B pattern using the precut spike and triangle pieces. Stitch on the straight solid lines, beginning and ending in the seam allowances. Trim the excess seam allowances between the pieces to ¼", but do not trim the seam allowances along the curved edges.

3. Join the A and B units to make a ring. Do not remove the foundation paper yet.

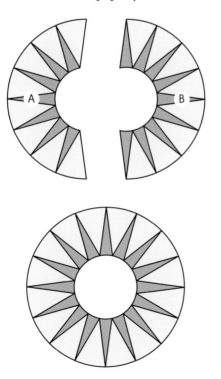

4. Repeat steps 1–3 to make 18 paper-pieced rings.

5. To make half blocks for the side setting triangles, select one set of group #2 pieces. Referring to step 2, paper piece one C pattern and one D pattern. Repeat to make five pairs of matching units.

6. To make quarter blocks for the corner setting triangles, use the group #3 pieces and refer to step 2 to paper piece the four E patterns.

Appliquéing the Paper-Pieced Units

Below are instructions for appliquéing the units. For details on the back-basting appliqué method Betsy used, see "Back-Basting and Reverse Appliqué" at right.

1. Follow steps 1–3 of "Back-Basting and Reverse Appliqué" to back-baste appliqué the center circle to the center opening of a paper-pieced ring.

2. Repeat step 1 with the remaining paper-pieced rings, half rings, and quarter rings.

3. Follow steps 4 and 5 of "Back-Basting and Reverse Appliqué" to reverse appliqué a ring to a background square. Remove the foundation paper. Press the unit. Carefully trim away the excess fabric from the outer edges of the triangle and spike pieces, leaving a ¼" seam allowance. Square up the unit to 12½" square. Make a total of 18 units.

4. In the same manner, appliqué each half circle to a cream side setting triangle and each quarter circle to a cream corner setting triangle. Do not trim the edges of the setting pieces.

Back-Basting and Reverse Appliqué

1. Place a 5" square that coordinates with the outer triangles of a sunburst ring over the center opening of the ring with both pieces right side up. Make sure the square covers the inner points of the outer triangle pieces; pin the square in place.

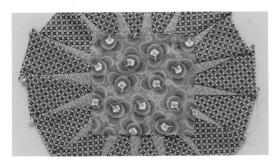

2. Working on the wrong (paper) side, machine baste on the stitching line of the inner circle. Add a row of basting stitches at least ½" from each side of the first stitching line to stabilize the square as you appliqué. (Note: basting is shown in red for visibility.) Remove the pins.

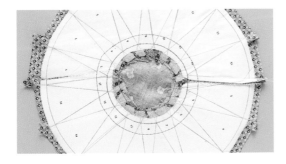

3. Turn the sunburst unit right side up and trace over the stitching line (the center ring of basting) with a fabric pencil. Clip into the square fabric ¼" *outside* the marked stitching line and make a cut about 2" long. Clip a few of the inner-circle basting stitches along the cut area and remove the clipped threads. Turn under the seam allowance of the circle along the marked line and hand appliqué the edge in place. Continue around the circle in this manner, clipping the square fabric, removing a few basting stitches, and turning under and appliquéing the edge in place. When the entire circle edge has been appliquéd in place, remove the basting stitches on each side of the finished edge and discard the excess fabric.

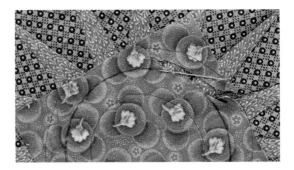

4. Fold a cream 13" square in half vertically and horizontally and lightly press the folds. Unfold the square and place it right side *down*. Place the ring, also right side down, on top of the square, aligning the spike points with the folds of the square; pin in place. Machine baste on the outer-circle seamline and ½" from both sides of the first ring of basting.

5. Turn the unit right side up and use a fabric marker to trace over the center ring of stitches. Carefully cut into the cream square ¼" from the *inside* of the traced seamline, making a cut about 2" long. Clip a few of the basting stitches on the outer-circle stitching line along the clipped area and remove them. Turn under the seam allowance of the cream fabric along the marked line and appliqué the edge in place. Continue trimming in this manner around the entire ring. When complete, trim the cream curved seam allowance to ¼".

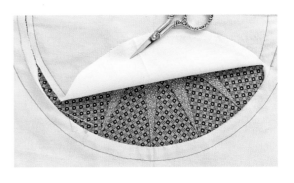

Making and Attaching the Frames

Betsy used paper-foundation piecing to make 1½" finished half-square-triangle units. (See "Cutting" on page 69.) If you prefer to use traditional piecing, follow step 1 below.

1. Draw a diagonal line from corner to corner on the wrong side of each cream 2⅜" square. Layer a marked cream square on top of a 2⅜" brown floral square, right sides together. Sew ¼" from each side of the marked line. Cut the squares apart on the marked line to make two half-square-triangle units. Press the seam allowances toward the brown print. Repeat to make a total 878 half-square-triangle units. Square up each unit to 2" x 2".

Make 878.

2. Sew the half-square-triangle units together side by side as shown to make framing strips A, B, and C (strips should be 12½"-long, 15½"-long, and 14"-long respectively). Make the number of strips indicated for each. Press the seam allowances toward the right.

Framing Strip A.
Make 36.

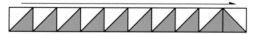

Framing Strip B.
Make 50.

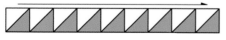

Framing Strip C.
Make 10.

3. Sew A framing strips to the sides of an appliquéd block unit as shown. Press the seam allowances toward the strips. Sew B framing strips to the top and bottom of the block unit as shown. Press

the seam allowances toward the strips. Repeat to make a total of 18 blocks.

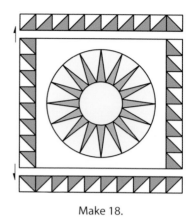

Make 18.

4. Sew a C framing strip to one short side of an appliquéd side setting triangle as shown, aligning the end of the strip with the triangle point. The strip will extend past the long edge. Press the seam allowances toward the strip. Add a B framing strip to the remaining short side of the triangle as shown. Press the seam allowances toward the strip. Repeat to make a total of 10 side setting triangles.

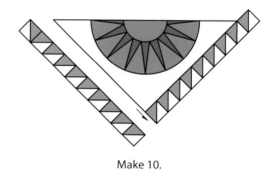

Make 10.

5. Center and sew a B framing strip to the long side of an appliquéd corner triangle. Press the seam allowances toward the strip. Repeat to make a total of four corner setting triangles.

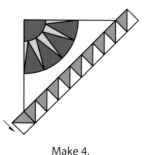

Make 4.

Assembling and Finishing the Quilt

For more details on quilting and finishing, go to ShopMartingale.com/HowtoQuilt.

1. Arrange the blocks and side setting triangles into six diagonal rows. Sew together the blocks and triangles in each row. (The triangle frames will extend beyond the block edges and will be trimmed later.) Press the seam allowances in alternate directions from row to row. Join the rows. Press the seam allowances away from the center row. Add the corner setting triangles. Press the seam allowances toward the corners.

2. Trim the quilt edges ¼" from the block points.

3. Cut and piece the backing so it's 4" larger than the quilt top on all sides. Layer the quilt top, batting, and backing; baste.

4. Quilt as desired. The quilt shown was machine quilted in a feathered wreath pattern.

5. Bind the quilt edges with the 2" x 42" brown strips.

Quilt assembly

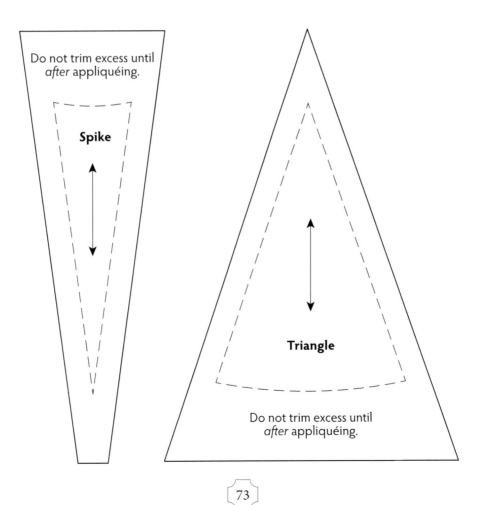

Do not trim excess until *after* appliquéing.

Spike

Triangle

Do not trim excess until *after* appliquéing.

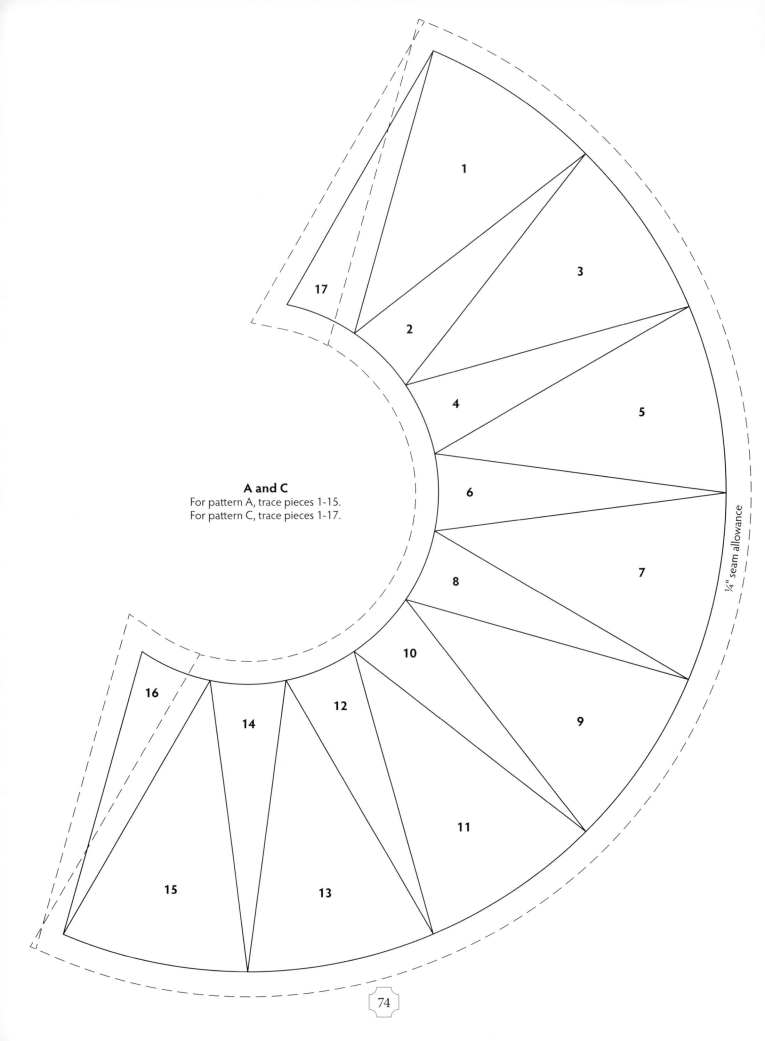

A and C
For pattern A, trace pieces 1-15.
For pattern C, trace pieces 1-17.

1

2

3

4

5

6

7

8

9

10

11

12

13

14

15

16

17

¼" seam allowance

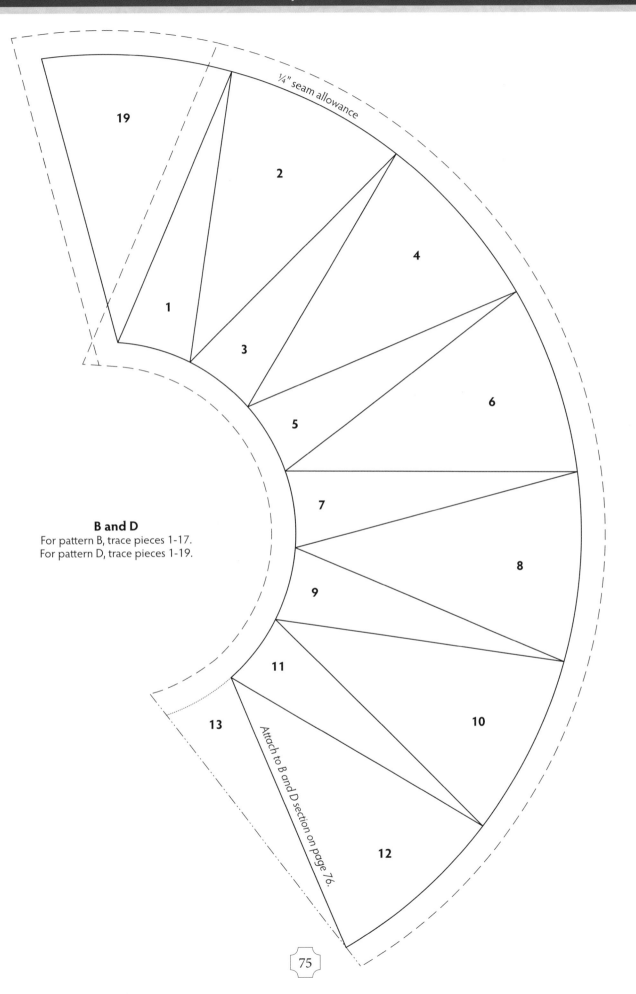

19

2

4

1

3

6

5

7

B and D
For pattern B, trace pieces 1-17.
For pattern D, trace pieces 1-19.

8

9

11

10

13

¼" seam allowance

Attach to B and D section on page 76.

12

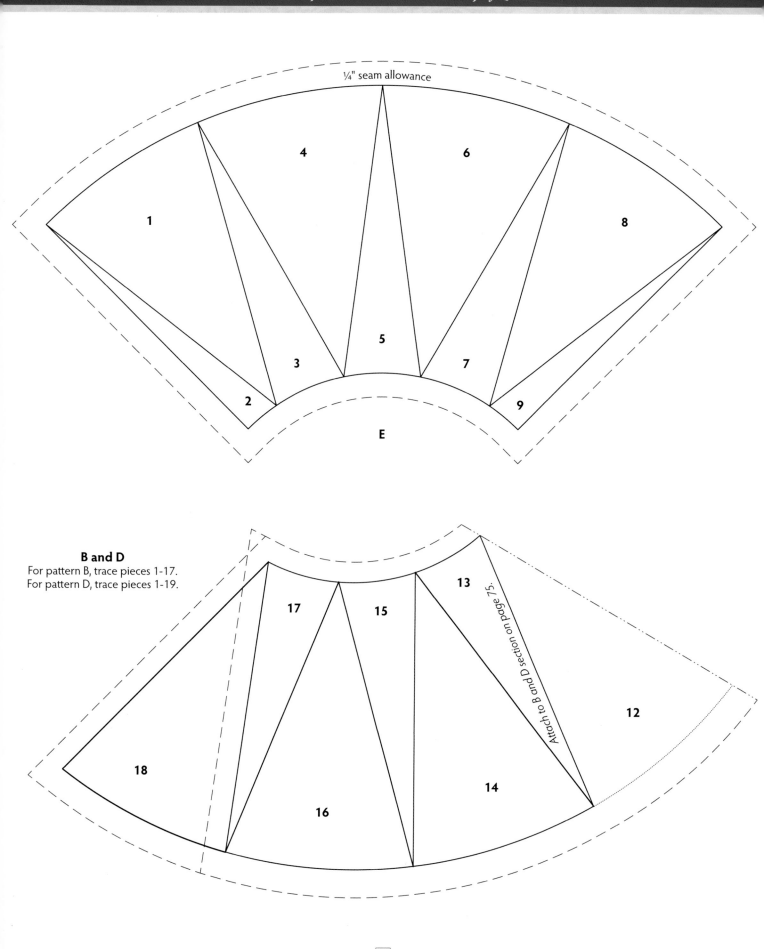

¼" seam allowance

4

6

1

8

5

3

7

2

9

E

B and D
For pattern B, trace pieces 1-17.
For pattern D, trace pieces 1-19.

17

15

13

Attach to B and D section on page 75.

12

18

16

14

Antique Sunburst

By Annette Plog; machine quilted by Sheri Mecom

FINISHED QUILT: 58½" x 75⅜"

Annette set the blocks side by side on point without sashing and used a large-scale print for the setting triangles and border.

The Olde Well

By Marilyn Mowry; machine quilted by Sheri Mecom

Finished Quilt: 60½" x 72½"

Marilyn alternated finished blocks with chintz print squares in this straight-row setting.

Chintz Sunburst

By Peggy Morton; machine quilted by Elizabeth A. Miller

FINISHED QUILT: 95½" x 110"

Peggy added 2½"-wide sashing strips and cornerstones between straight-set blocks and finished with a 10"-wide fussy-cut border.

Chancing upon a very unusual Antique Star quilt in Houston (shown on page 91), Betsy purchased the quilt and it became our inspiration for a unique Feathered Star block exchange. Because the antique quilt had a shirting print in the large center square, and some members preferred a darker center, we gave both options for the exchange. Almost everyone departed from the antique quilt and went with a darker center.

Delectable Feathered Star

By Sue Troyan; machine quilted by Sylvia Thompson

FINISHED QUILT: 80½" x 97¾"
FINISHED BLOCK: 14¼" x 14¼"

Sue arranged Feathered Star blocks in a straight setting using a single shirting print for the sashing and border to tie them all together. She used madder prints from her own collection to create the small stars at the sashing intersections.

Materials

Yardage is based on 42"-wide fabric. Fat quarters measure approximately 18" x 21". Chubby sixteenths measure approximately 9" x 10½".

In the featured quilt, some block backgrounds are scrappy. For ease of construction, the instructions have been simplified so that each block uses one shirting print for all background pieces.

20 fat quarters of assorted light shirting prints for block backgrounds and feather-point units

3 yards *total* of assorted madder and brown prints for block centers, inner star points, and sashing stars

2 yards of light shirting print for sashing and border

20 chubby sixteenths of assorted accent prints for feather-point units (the featured quilt used madders, browns, blues, golds, and pinks)

⅝ yard of brown print for border

⅔ yard of light shirting print for binding

8 yards of fabric for backing

89" x 106" piece of batting

Cutting

CUTTING FOR BLOCKS

The cutting instructions are for one block. For each block, select one shirting print (shirting #1) and one accent print for the feather units, a different shirting print (shirting #2) for the background, one madder or brown print (#1) for the center square, and a different madder or brown print (#2) for the inner-star points. Repeat the instructions to cut the pieces for 20 blocks. Keep the pieces for each block together.

From shirting #1, cut:

12 squares, 2" x 2"

4 squares, 1½" x 1½"

From the accent print, cut:

12 squares 2" x 2"

4 squares, 1⅞" x 1⅞"; cut each square in half diagonally to yield 8 triangles

From shirting #2, cut:

1 square, 7" x 7"; cut into quarters diagonally to yield 4 triangles

4 squares, 4¾" x 4¾"

From the madder or brown print #1, cut:

1 square, 6¼" x 6¼"

From madder or brown print #2, cut:

4 squares, 3¾" x 3¾"; cut each square in half diagonally to yield 8 triangles

CUTTING FOR REMAINING PIECES

From 1 madder print, cut:

8 squares, 2" x 2"

From the remaining assorted madder and brown prints, cut a *total* of:

12 squares, 3½" x 3½"

96 squares, 2" x 2"

From the assorted shirting prints, cut a *total* of:

31 rectangles, 3½" x 14¾"

From the shirting print for sashing and border, cut:

2 strips, 4½" x 42"; crosscut into:

4 squares, 4½" x 4½"

8 rectangles, 3½" x 4½"

16 strips, 3½" x 42"

2 squares, 4" x 4"

From the brown print for border, cut:

8 strips, 1½" x 42"

2 squares, 4" x 4"

8 squares, 2" x 2"

From the shirting print for binding, cut:

10 strips, 2" x 42"

Making the Feathered Star Blocks

1. Select the pieces cut for one block.

2. Draw a diagonal line from corner to corner on the wrong side of each 2" shirting square. Lay a marked square on top of a 2" accent square, right sides together. Sew ¼" from each side of the marked line. Cut apart the squares on the marked line to make two half-square-triangle units. Repeat to make a total of 24 units. Press the seam allowances toward the accent print. Square up each unit to 1½" x 1½".

Make 24.

3. Sew three half-square-triangle units and one accent triangle together as shown to make unit A. Press the seam allowances as indicated. Repeat to make a total of four A units. Join three half-square-triangle units, one accent triangle, and one 1½" shirting square as shown to make unit B. Press the seam allowances as indicated. Repeat to make a total of four B units.

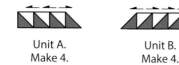

Unit A.
Make 4.

Unit B.
Make 4.

4. Sew one A unit to one short edge of a shirting triangle, aligning the half-square-triangle end with the point of the triangle. Press the seam allowances toward the large triangle. Join a unit B strip to the opposite short edge. Press the seam allowances toward the large triangle. Repeat to make a total of four units.

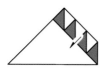

Make 4.

5. Sew two brown or madder triangles to each unit from step 4. Press the seam allowances toward the triangles. Each side unit should measure 4¾" x 6¼".

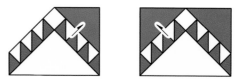

Make 4.

6. Arrange the 6¼" madder or brown square, the shirting #2 squares, and the pieced side units from step 5 into three horizontal rows as shown. Sew the units in each row together. Press the seam allowances away from the step 5 units. Join the rows. The block should measure 14¾" square including the seam allowances.

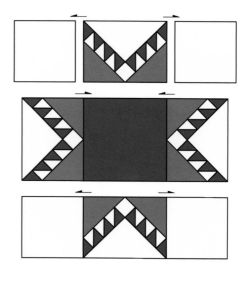

7. To maintain the block points, clip the seam allowances ¼" from each side of the seam intersections. Press the seam allowances away from the step 5 units and press the seam intersections open.

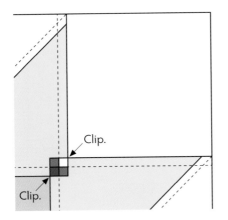

8. Repeat steps 1–7 to make a total of 20 Feathered Star blocks.

Making the Sashing

1. Draw a diagonal line from corner to corner on the wrong side of the 96 assorted madder and brown 2" squares.

2. Layer a marked square on one corner of a shirting 3½" x 14¾" rectangle as shown, right sides together. Sew on the marked line. Trim the excess ¼" from the stitching line. Press the seam allowances toward the madder or brown square. Repeat on the adjacent corner at the same end of the rectangle. Repeat to make a total of 14 single-point sashing units.

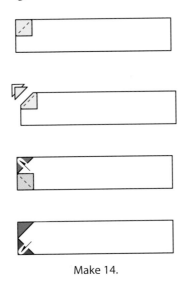

Make 14.

3. Repeat step 2 on both ends of the remaining 3½" x 14¾" shirting rectangles to make 17 double-point sashing units.

Make 17.

Assembling and Finishing the Quilt

For more details on quilting and finishing, go to ShopMartingale.com/HowtoQuilt.

1. Refer to the quilt assembly diagram on page 87 to arrange the blocks, the single- and double-pointed sashing units, and 12 madder or brown 3½" squares in nine horizontal rows. Join the pieces in each row. Press the seam allowances toward the sashing units. Join the rows. Press the seam allowances toward the sashing rows.

2. To make the border corner squares, draw a diagonal line from corner to corner on the wrong side of each border shirting 4" square. Lay a marked square on top of a 4" border brown square, right sides together. Sew ¼" from each side of the marked line. Cut apart the squares on the marked line to make two half-square-triangle units. Repeat to make a total of four units. Press the seam allowances toward the brown print. Trim each unit to 3½" x 3½".

Make 4.

3. Draw a diagonal line from corner to corner on the remaining eight 2" madder squares and 2" brown squares. Place a marked madder square on the upper-left corner of a 3½" x 4½" shirting rectangle. Sew on the marked line. Trim ¼" from the stitching line. Press the seam allowances

toward the corner. Repeat on the adjacent corner of the same end with a marked brown square. Repeat to make a total of four units. In the same manner, make an additional four units, reversing the position of the madder and brown squares.

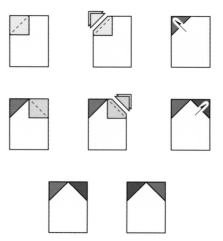

Make 4 of each.

4. Lay out one 4½" shirting square, one step 2 unit, and one of each of the step 3 units in two horizontal rows as shown. Sew the units together in rows. Press the seam allowances as indicated. Join the rows. Press the seam allowances toward the top row. Repeat to make a total of four border corner squares that each measure 7½" square including seam allowances.

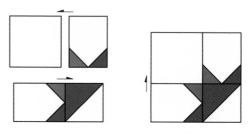

Make 4.

5. Sew the shirting 3½" x 42" strips together end to end to make one long strip. From the pieced strip, cut four 83¾"-long strips and four 66½"-long strips.

6. Sew the 1½" x 42" brown strips together end to end to make one long strip. From the pieced strip, cut two 83¾"-long strips and two 66½"-long strips.

7. Sew the 83¾"-long shirting strips to both long edges of an 83¾"-long brown strip. Press the seam allowances toward the brown strip. Repeat to make a total of two pieced border strips. Sew these strips to the sides of the quilt top. Press the seam allowances toward the border strips.

8. Sew the 66½"-long shirting strips to both long edges of a 66½"-long brown strip. Press the seam allowances toward the brown strip. Repeat to make a total of two border strips. Sew a border corner square from step 4 to the end of each of these strips. Press the seam allowances toward the

border strip. Join the strips to the top and bottom of the quilt top. Press the seam allowances toward the border strips.

9. Cut and piece the backing so it's 4" larger than the quilt top on all sides. Layer the quilt top, batting, and backing; baste.

10. Quilt as desired. The quilt shown was machine quilted with parallel lines in the blocks and feathers in the sashing. The block centers feature feathered wreaths.

11. Bind the quilt edges with the 2" x 42" shirting strips.

Quilt assembly

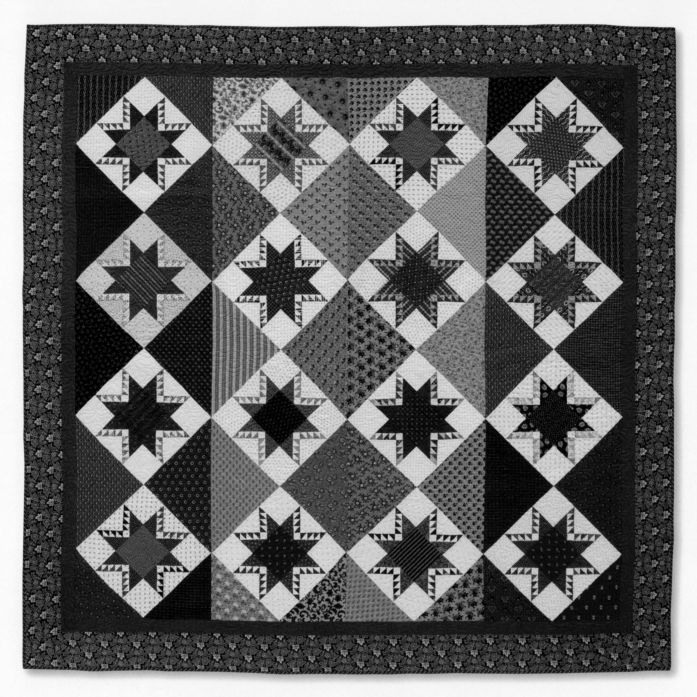

It Matters with Madder

By Jean Johnson; machine quilted by Sheri Mecom

FINISHED QUILT: 95" x 95"

Jean set the blocks on point, using a variety of madder and brown prints for setting triangles. To replicate, you'll need 14½" triangles to make four vertical columns with four blocks each. The inner border is 2" wide and the outer border is 5" wide.

Montana Stars

By Linda Cordell; machine quilted by Dana Goyer

Finished Quilt: 84" x 107¾"

Linda's blocks are set on point with 2½"-wide sashing and cornerstones. Notice that the setting triangles are cut from strip-pieced fabric (blue, red, blue) giving the impression of an inner border. The border is 4½" wide.

Autumn Feathered Star

Pieced and hand quilted by Ann Jernigan

FINISHED QUILT: 57¼" x 74½"

Ann used half-square-triangle units in the corners of the blocks to give them an octagon shape when set with 3½"-wide sashing and borders of the same dark fabric used in the quilts' corners.

Antique Feathered Star

Owned by Betsy Chutchian

FINISHED QUILT: 77" x 88"

Unusual by today's standards, this intricately pieced quilt top features light-colored centers in the Feathered Star blocks and dark pieces on both sides of the pieced sections, giving the overall appearance of a Nine Patch block.

For the Ohio Star exchange, we were drawn in by the sweet simplicity of many early 1800s quilts, which frequently featured Ohio Star blocks. In settings from simple to on-point to more complex, the tiny 4½" star is the standout feature.

Star Crossed

By Sonja Kraus; machine quilted by Sheri Mecom

FINISHED QUILT: 63½" x 79"
FINISHED BLOCK: 11" x 11"

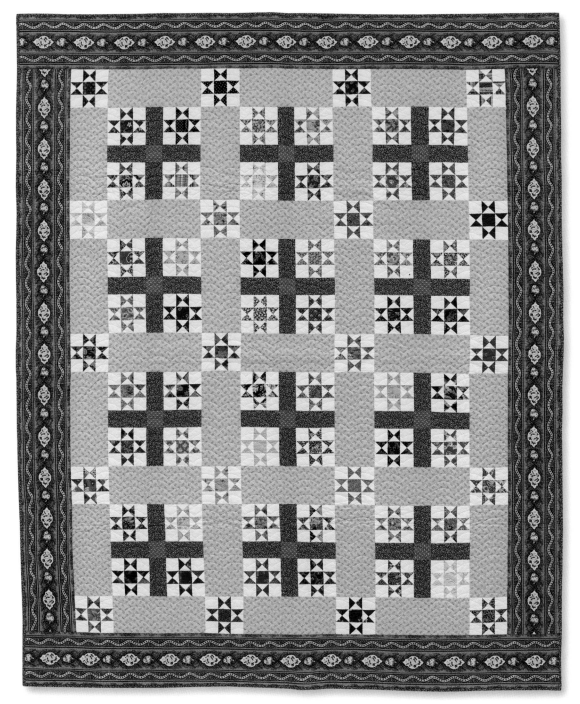

Intrigued by a quilt in the book Quilts of Virginia 1607–1899 *(Schiffer Publishing, 2007), Sonja set four stars in sashed quadrants to create her blocks. Individual stars create a unified setting when used for the sashing cornerstones in the quilt design.*

Materials

Yardage is based on 42"-wide fabric.

2⅛ yards of brown-and-gold lengthwise stripe for border

2 yards of cream solid for Ohio Star backgrounds

1¾ yards of gold print for quilt sashing

1⅓ yards *total* of assorted dark prints for Ohio Stars

1 yard of blue print for block sashing and binding

⅛ yard of brown print for block sashing cornerstones

5⅓ yards of fabric for backing

72" x 87" piece of batting

Cutting

From the cream solid, cut:

11 strips, 3" x 42"; crosscut into 136 squares, 3" x 3"

14 strips, 2" x 42"; crosscut into 272 squares, 2" x 2"

From the assorted dark prints, cut 68 sets of:

2 squares, 3" x 3"*

1 square, 2" x 2"*

From the blue print, cut:

6 strips, 2½" x 42"; crosscut into 48 rectangles, 2½" x 5"

8 strips, 2" x 42"

From the brown print, cut:

12 squares, 2½" x 2½"

From the gold print, cut:

31 rectangles, 5" x 11½"

*Cut all 3 squares in each set from the same print.

Assembling the Ohio Star Units and Blocks

1. Draw a diagonal line from corner to corner on the wrong side of each 3" cream square.

2. Select one set of dark squares. Layer a marked cream square on top of each 3" dark square, right sides together. Sew ¼" from each side of the marked lines. Cut apart the squares on the marked lines to make four half-square-triangle units. Press the seam allowances toward the dark print.

Make 4.

3. Layer two units from step 2 right sides together with the dark sides opposing each other. Draw a diagonal line from corner to corner in the opposite direction as the seams. Sew ¼" from each side of the marked line. Cut apart the squares on the marked line to make two quarter-square-triangle units. Press the seam allowances in one direction. Repeat with the remaining two units to make a total of four quarter-square-triangle units. Square up each unit to 2" x 2".

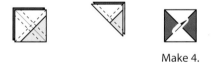

Make 4.

4. Arrange the four quarter-square-triangle units, the 2" dark square, and four 2" cream squares in three horizontal rows as shown. Sew the pieces in each row together. Press the seam allowances toward the squares. Join the rows to make a 5"-square Ohio Star unit, including seam allowances.

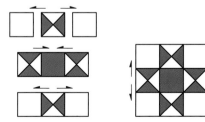

5. To maintain the block points, clip the seam allowances ¼" from each side of the seam intersections, and then press the seam allowances away from the quarter-square-triangle units.

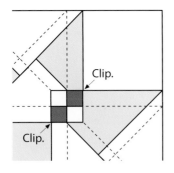

6. Repeat steps 2–5 to make a total of 68 Ohio Star units.

7. Arrange four Ohio Star units, four 2½" x 5" blue sashing rectangles, and one 2½" brown square in three horizontal rows as shown. Sew the pieces in each row together. Press the seam allowances toward the sashing rectangles. Join the rows. Press the seam allowances toward the center row. Repeat to make a total of 12 blocks. Each block should measure 11½" square, including seam allowances.

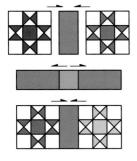
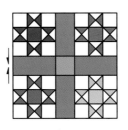

Make 12.

Assembling and Finishing the Quilt

For more details on quilting and finishing, go to ShopMartingale.com/HowtoQuilt.

1. Refer to the quilt assembly diagram above right to lay out the blocks, the remaining 20 Ohio Star units, and the 5" x 11½" gold sashing rectangles in nine horizontal rows as shown. Sew the pieces in each row together. Press the seam allowances toward the sashing rectangles. Join the rows. Press the seam allowances toward the sashing rows.

2. Measure the quilt top through the center from top to bottom. From the *lengthwise grain* of the border stripe, fussy cut two 6½"-wide strips (centering the same part of the stripe motif in each one) to the length measured. Sew the strips to the sides of the quilt top. Press the seam allowances toward the border strips. Measure the quilt top through the center from side to side, including the borders just added. From the *lengthwise grain* of the remaining border stripe, fussy cut two 6½"-wide strips in the same manner to the length measured. Join these strips to the top and bottom of the quilt top. Press the seam allowances toward the border strips.

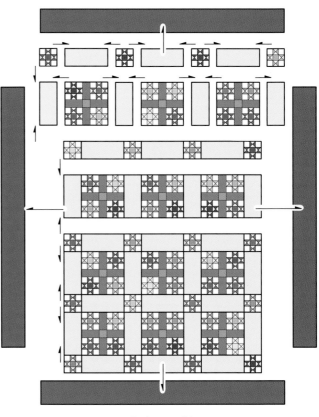

Quilt assembly

3. Cut and piece the backing so it's 4" larger than the quilt top on all sides. Layer the quilt top, batting, and backing; baste.

4. Quilt as desired. The quilt shown was machine quilted with a repeating scallop pattern.

5. Bind the quilt edges with the 2" x 42" blue strips.

Pheasant Stars

By Mary Freeman; quilted by Gail Rowland

FINISHED QUILT: 63" x 72"

Mary alternated Ohio Star blocks with simple pieced 4½"-finished Snowball blocks in a straight setting. Notice in the outer perimeter of blocks, Mary used squares of the border fabric in place of the Snowballs. The pink inner border is ½" wide and the outer border is 6" wide.

Show Me a Star

By Julia Berggren; machine quilted by Sheri Mecom

FINISHED QUILT: 54" x 71¼"

*Julia used a simple straight setting, separating the blocks
with 1¼"-wide sashing. The border is 6" wide.*

Stars and Hexagons

By Peggy Morton; machine quilted by Elizabeth A. Miller

FINISHED QUILT: 91½" x 100½"

*A center chintz panel is surrounded by borders of Ohio Star blocks and
English paper-pieced hexagons that alternate with chintz borders of varying
widths in a medallion setting. The outer border is 13¾" wide.*

Photos of antique quilts from the mid-19th century led us to use one light-cream solid fabric for the sunflower points to unify the blocks. The resulting quilts were quite varied in settings and reminiscent of the antique quilts we love. For this exchange we used From Marti Michell acrylic templates; the resulting blocks were accurate and easy to make and produced beautiful results. Patterns to make your own templates are included if you choose not to purchase the acrylic set.

Sunflowers and Flying Geese

By Arlene Heintz; machine quilted by Julia Mason

FINISHED QUILT: 74¾" x 98"

FINISHED BLOCK: 13½" x 13½"

Arlene accented the blocks with a scrappy setting. She carefully chose a different print for each block background so that every one is unique. Each block was then framed with a scrappy flying-geese sashing. Set on point with a large floral print, every block is a fabric lover's scrappy wonder.

Materials

Yardage is based on 42"-wide fabric. Fat quarters measure approximately 18" x 21". Fat eighths measure approximately 9" x 21".

1 fat quarter *each* of 18 assorted dark prints for block backgrounds (dark #1)

1 fat eighth *each* of 18 assorted dark prints for sunflower appliqué B diamonds and center circle (dark #2)

1 fat eighth *each* of 18 assorted medium prints for sunflower appliqué outer C triangles (medium #1)

2¼ yards *total* of assorted medium and dark prints for pieced sashing (medium #2)

3 yards of wine print for setting triangles and binding

2¼ yards *total* of assorted light prints for pieced sashing

1⅓ yards of cream solid for sunflower appliqué inner A triangles

7½ yards of fabric for backing

83" x 106" piece of batting

From Marti Michell Perfect Patchwork Templates Set F *OR* template plastic

Cutting

If you're not using the From Marti Michell acrylic templates, trace the A, B, and C shapes on page 107 onto template plastic and cut them out. Be sure to transfer the alignment dots and grain-line arrows to each template. Use the templates to cut the pieces from the fabrics indicated, aligning the grain-line arrows with the fabric grain line. A 28 mm rotary cutter works well to cut around the acrylic templates, or you can use a mechanical pencil to trace the shapes onto the fabrics and cut them out with scissors.

CUTTING FOR BLOCKS

The cutting instructions are for one block. For each block select one dark #1 print for the block background, one dark #2 print for the B diamonds and

appliquéd center circle, and one medium #1 print for the C outer triangles. The A pieces are all cut from the cream solid. You can cut these pieces for one block at a time or cut all the pieces at once. To add variety to the blocks, reverse the position of the dark and medium fabrics or use a different dark print for the center circle than for the B pieces. Repeat the instructions to cut the pieces for 18 blocks. Keep the pieces for each block together.

From dark #1, cut:

1 square, 14½" x 14½"

From the cream solid, cut:

16 A pieces (or 288 total)

From dark #2, cut:

16 B pieces

1 center circle

From medium #1, cut:

16 C pieces

CUTTING FOR REMAINING PIECES

From the assorted light prints, cut a *total* of:

432 squares, 2⅜" x 2⅜"; cut each square in half diagonally to yield 864 triangles

From medium #2, cut a *total* of:

108 squares, 4¼" x 4¼"; cut each square into quarters diagonally to yield 432 triangles

124 squares, 2" x 2"

From the wine print, cut:

9 strips, 2" x 42"

3 squares, 25" x 25"; cut each square into quarters diagonally to yield 12 side setting triangles (you'll use 10 and have 2 left over)*

2 squares, 15" x 15"; cut each square in half diagonally to yield 4 corner setting triangles*

These triangles are cut oversized and will be trimmed after the quilt top is assembled.

Making the Sunflower Blocks

1. Select the pieces for one block and mark the alignment dots on each A, B, and C fabric piece.

2. Sew an A piece to the lower-right edge of a B piece, matching the alignment dots and sewing from raw edge to raw edge. Press the seam allowances toward the A piece. Repeat to make a total of 16 units.

Make 16.

3. With the AB unit on top, join a C piece to the upper right edge of the B piece of each unit from step 3, sewing from the center dot to the outer edge. Press the seam allowances toward the C pieces.

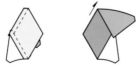

Make 16.

4. Sew the units from step 4 together in pairs, sewing from the center dot to the outer edge of the C piece and then from the outer edge of the B piece to the center dot. Join the pairs to make quarter units, and then join these units in pairs to make two half units. Sew the halves together to complete the outer ring.

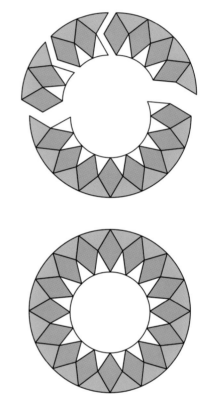

5. Using your favorite method, appliqué the center circle to the center opening of the ring. See "Back-Basting and Reverse Appliqué" on page 71 to see how the 19th-Century Patchwork Divas appliquéd their blocks so precisely.

6. Fold the dark #1 background square in half horizontally and vertically and lightly press the folds to mark the center. Repeat with the sunflower appliqué. With right sides up and the centers matching, appliqué the sunflower to the background to complete the block. Square up the block to 14" x 14".

7. Repeat steps 1–6 to make a total of 18 blocks.

Making the Sashing

1. Using the assorted light and medium #2 triangles, sew light triangles to both short sides of a medium #2 triangle to make a flying-geese unit. Press the seam allowances toward the corners. Repeat to make a total of 432 flying-geese units. Trim each unit to 2" x 3½".

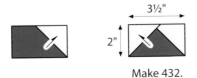

Make 432.

2. Sew nine flying-geese units together as shown to make a sashing strip. Press the seam allowances toward the points. Repeat to make a total of 48 sashing strips. The sashing strips should measure 3½" x 14".

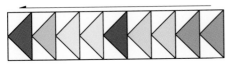

Make 48.

3. Lay out four 2" medium #2 squares in two rows of two squares each. Sew the squares in each row together. Press the seam allowances in alternating directions. Join the rows. Press the seam allowances in one direction. Repeat to make a total of 31 sashing cornerstone units, each measuring 3½" square, including seam allowances.

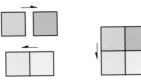

Make 31.

Assembling and Finishing the Quilt

For more details on quilting and finishing, go to ShopMartingale.com/HowtoQuilt.

1. Refer to the quilt assembly diagram below to lay out the blocks, sashing strips, sashing cornerstones, and wine side setting triangles in 13 diagonal rows. Sew the pieces in each row together. Press the seam allowances toward the blocks and side setting triangles. Join the rows.

Press the seam allowances away from the center row. Add the corner setting triangles. Press the seam allowances toward the corners.

2. Cut and piece the backing so it's 4" larger than the quilt top on all sides. Layer the quilt top, batting, and backing; baste.

3. Quilt as desired. The quilt shown was machine quilted with diamond crosshatching in the corner triangles, shallow scallops in the flying-geese sashing, and feathers around each circle.

4. Bind the quilt edges with the 2" x 42" wine strips.

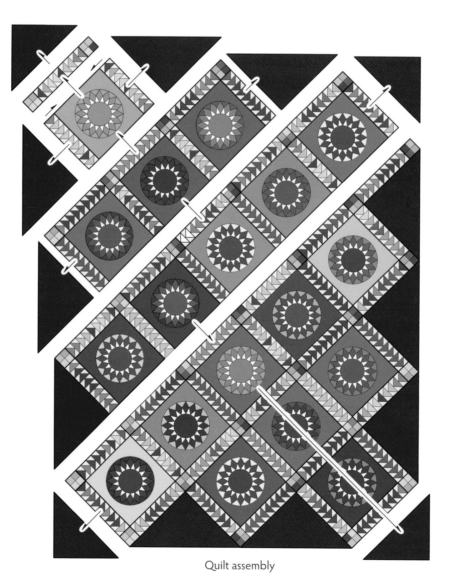

Quilt assembly

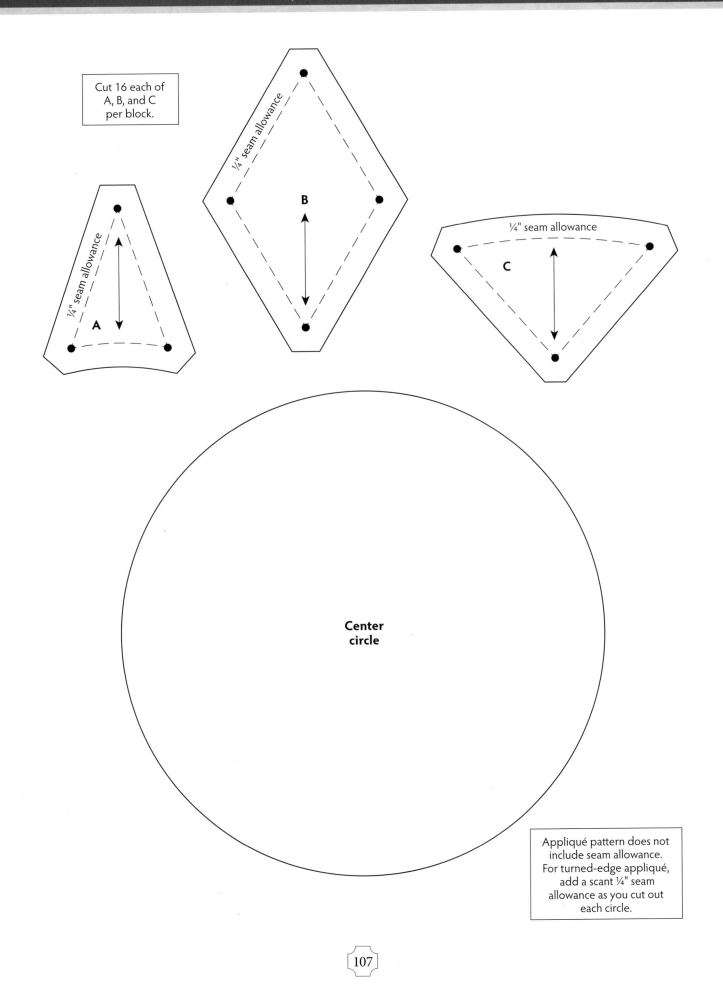

Cut 16 each of
A, B, and C
per block.

¼" seam allowance

B

¼" seam allowance

A

¼" seam allowance

C

¼" seam allowance

Center
circle

Appliqué pattern does not
include seam allowance.
For turned-edge appliqué,
add a scant ¼" seam
allowance as you cut out
each circle.

My First Love

By Linda Cordell; machine quilted by Julia Mason

FINISHED QUILT: 76⅞" x 76⅞"

Linda's on-point blocks are accented with broderie perse appliquéd motifs in the center square and setting triangles. For this setting, the framed center square needs to be 40½"-finished for the surrounding blocks to fit.

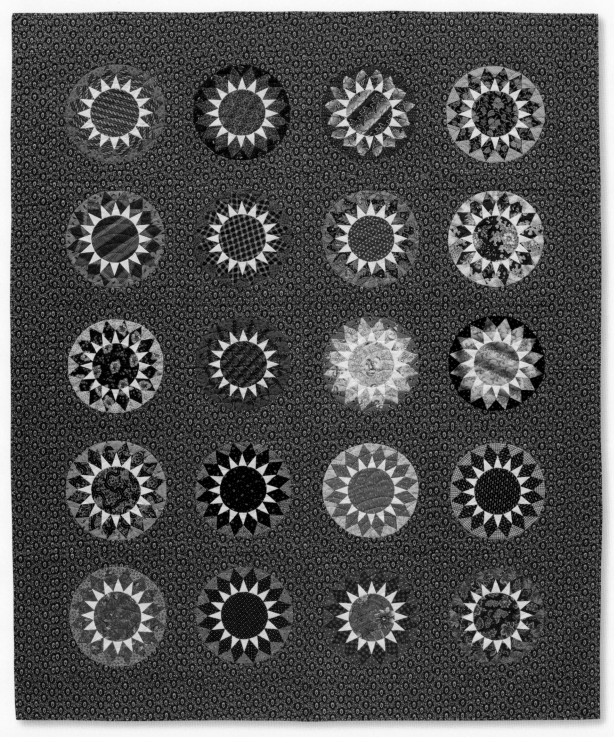

Fields of Color

By Carol Staehle; machine quilted by Sheri Mecom

FINISHED QUILT: 60½" x 73½"

Carol used a single background fabric for all of the blocks and trimmed them to finish at 13" square. She set them side by side with a matching 4"-wide border.

Toby's Troubles

By Ann Jernigan; hand quilted by Ruthie Taylor

FINISHED QUILT: 72" x 91"

*Ann's blocks, trimmed to finish at 12" square, are set on point with
1½"-wide sashing. A 6½"-wide border completes the quilt.*

Our thanks and deep appreciation go to the 19th-Century Patchwork Divas, whose creativity abounds and serves as a constant source of inspiration. Their generosity and willingness to share their talent and beautiful quilts made this book possible.

Thanks also to Rhonda Weddle and Renita Hall for their typing assistance.

And a huge thank-you to the Martingale team who made working on this book a pleasure.

Back row, left to right: Sonja Kraus, Deb Otto, Julia Berggren, Mary Freeman, Linda Cordell, Carol Staehle

Middle row: Diana Petterson, Stacey Barrington, Ann Jernigan, Jean Johnson, Arlene Heintz, Annette Plog

Seated: Betsy Chutchian, Janet Henderson, Marilyn Mowry

Not Shown: Betty Edgell, Alice Harvey, Wanda Hetrick, Karen Hodges, Peggy Morton, Karen Roxburgh, Charlene Seifert, Sue Troyan, and Ramona Williams

Quiltmakers

Stacey Barrington, Seguin, Texas
Julia Berggren, Arlington, Texas
Linda Cordell, Mathis, Texas
Betsy Chutchian, Grand Prairie, Texas
Betty Edgell, Colleyville, Texas
Mary Freeman, Schertz, Texas
Arlene Heintz, Waxahachie, Texas
Janet Henderson, Fort Worth, Texas
Ann Jernigan, Arlington, Texas
Jean Johnson, Murphy, Texas
Sonja Kraus, Dalworthington Gardens, Texas
Peggy Morton, Boerne, Texas
Marilyn Mowry, Irving, Texas

Deb Otto, Euless, Texas
Diana Petterson, Dallas, Texas
Annette Plog, Arlington, Texas
Karen Roxburgh, Bailey, Colorado
Carol Staehle, Arlington, Texas
Sue Troyan, Virginia Beach, Virginia
Ramona Williams, Missouri City, Texas

Also Divas

Alice Harvey, Arlington, Texas
Wanda Hetrick, Arlington, Texas
Karen Hodges, Syracuse, Utah
Charlene Seifert, Arlington, Texas

Quilters

Lera Borden, Boerne, Texas
Linda Carlson, Copperas Cove, Texas
Melba Drennan, Pearland, Texas
Dana Goyer, Euless, Texas
Julia Mason, Corpus Christi, Texas
Sheri Mecom, Bedford, Texas
Rita Meyerhoff, Arvada, Colorado
Elizabeth A. Miller, Cashton, Wisconsin
Gail Rowland, Spring, Texas
Dawn Smith, Grapevine, Texas
Ruthie Taylor, Kissimmee, Florida
Sylvia Thompson, Newport News, Virginia
Sandy Towey, Schertz, Texas

Betsy Chutchian

Betsy developed a passionate interest in fabric, quilts, sewing, and history as a child.

After graduation from the University of Texas at Arlington in 1980, Betsy received an antique quilt top made by her paternal great grandmother and great-aunt and taught herself to quilt. She began teaching quiltmaking in 1990 and continues to enjoy teaching and sharing her passion for reproducing 19th-century quilts.

Betsy is the author of four books and coauthor of two others; this is her first book published by Martingale. She is also the cofounder of the 19th-Century Patchwork Divas and a fabric designer for Moda.

Betsy and her husband, Steve, live in Grand Prairie, Texas.

Carol Staehle

Carol's love of needlework began when she was a young girl with simple embroidery and cross-stitch. A sewing class at age 12 was her first adventure with a sewing machine. That interest lasted for decades until the mid 1980s when she took her first quiltmaking class. Making clothing suddenly took a backseat to making quilts, which has occupied her free time for the last 30 plus years.

Carol feels fortunate to have a quilt from each of her grandmothers, which she will pass on to her granddaughter, who has enjoyed making her first quilt at age eight.

Prior to moving to Texas in 1987, Carol had taught junior high language arts in Michigan and Iowa and high school English in Ohio.

An award-winning quiltmaker, she taught the "It's Okay" class and other quiltmaking classes at the local Arlington quilt shop for many years. Currently she leads a bimonthly club at Cabbage Rose Quilting and Fabrics in Fort Worth.

Carol and her family live in Arlington, Texas.